The Kentucky Bicentennial Bookshelf
Sponsored by

KENTUCKY HISTORICAL EVENTS CELEBRATION COMMISSION
KENTUCKY FEDERATION OF WOMEN'S CLUBS

and Contributing Sponsors

AMERICAN FEDERAL SAVINGS & LOAN ASSOCIATION
ARMCO STEEL CORPORATION, ASHLAND WORKS
A. ARNOLD & SON TRANSFER & STORAGE CO., INC. / ASHLAND OIL, INC.
BAILEY MINING COMPANY, BYPRO, KENTUCKY / BEGLEY DRUG COMPANY
J. WINSTON COLEMAN, JR. / CONVENIENT INDUSTRIES OF AMERICA, INC.
IN MEMORY OF MR. AND MRS. J. SHERMAN COOPER BY THEIR CHILDREN
CORNING GLASS WORKS FOUNDATION / MRS. CLORA CORRELL
THE COURIER-JOURNAL AND THE LOUISVILLE TIMES
COVINGTON TRUST & BANKING COMPANY
MR. AND MRS. GEORGE P. CROUNSE / GEORGE E. EVANS, JR.
FARMERS BANK & CAPITAL TRUST COMPANY / FISHER-PRICE TOYS, MURRAY
MARY PAULINE FOX, M.D., IN HONOR OF CHLOE GIFFORD
MARY A. HALL, M.D., IN HONOR OF PAT LEE,
JANICE HALL & AND MARY ANN FAULKNER
OSCAR HORNSBY INC. / OFFICE PRODUCTS DIVISION IBM CORPORATION
JERRY'S RESTAURANTS / ROBERT B. JEWELL
LEE S. JONES / KENTUCKIANA GIRL SCOUT COUNCIL
KENTUCKY BANKERS ASSOCIATION / KENTUCKY COAL ASSOCIATION, INC.
THE KENTUCKY JOCKEY CLUB, INC. / THE LEXINGTON WOMAN'S CLUB
LINCOLN INCOME LIFE INSURANCE COMPANY
LORILLARD A DIVISION OF LOEW'S THEATRES, INC.
METROPOLITAN WOMAN'S CLUB OF LEXINGTON / BETTY HAGGIN MOLLOY
MUTUAL FEDERAL SAVINGS & LOAN ASSOCIATION
NATIONAL INDUSTRIES, INC. / RAND MCNALLY & COMPANY
PHILIP MORRIS, INCORPORATED / MRS. VICTOR SAMS
SHELL OIL COMPANY, LOUISVILLE
SOUTH CENTRAL BELL TELEPHONE COMPANY
SOUTHERN BELLE DAIRY CO. INC.
STANDARD OIL COMPANY (KENTUCKY)
STANDARD PRINTING CO., H. M. KESSLER, PRESIDENT
STATE BANK & TRUST COMPANY, RICHMOND
THOMAS INDUSTRIES INC. / TIP TOP COAL CO., INC.
MARY L. WISS, M.D. / YOUNGER WOMAN'S CLUB OF ST. MATTHEWS

LUKE PRYOR BLACKBURN
Portrait by M. Marschell.
Courtesy of Kentucky Historical Society

LUKE PRYOR BLACKBURN

Physician, Governor, Reformer

NANCY DISHER BAIRD

THE UNIVERSITY PRESS OF KENTUCKY

Research for The Kentucky Bicentennial Bookshelf
is assisted by a grant from the
National Endowment for the Humanities.
Views expressed in the Bookshelf do not
necessarily represent those of the Endowment.

Library of Congress Cataloging in Publication Data

Baird, Nancy Disher.
    Luke Pryor Blackburn, physician, governor, reformer.

    (The Kentucky Bicentennial bookshelf)
    Includes bibliographical references.
    1. Blackburn, Luke Pryor, 1816-1887. 2. Prisons—
Kentucky—History. 3. Public health—Kentucky—History.
4. Kentucky—Politics and government—1865-1950.
5. Kentucky—Governors—Biography. 6. Physicians—
Kentucky—Biography. I. Title. II. Series.
F456.B5B34   976.9'04'0924 [B]   79-888
ISBN 0-8131-0248-0

Scholarly publisher for the Commonwealth,
serving Berea College, Centre College of Kentucky,
Eastern Kentucky University, The Filson Club,
Georgetown College, Kentucky Historical Society,
Kentucky State University, Morehead State University,
Murray State University, Northern Kentucky University,
Transylvania University, University of Kentucky,
University of Louisville, and Western Kentucky University.

Editorial and Sales Offices: Lexington, Kentucky 40506

Contents

To my parents

Preface

THE DIVERSE backgrounds of Kentucky's governors include careers in law, religion, agriculture, education, and the military. Only one governor, Luke Pryor Blackburn, has brought to the executive office knowledge in medicine and public health matters. During his medical career Blackburn won acclaim as the hero of numerous cholera and yellow fever epidemics but received condemnation for his attempt to practice germ warfare during the Civil War. Humane but politically unwise efforts to change Kentucky's penal system characterized his governorship. His determined crusade in behalf of the commonwealth's convicts brought about the first major post-Civil War reforms in Kentucky, yet rendered him odious to professional politicians of the era. In 1972, eighty-five years after his death, the state officially recognized Blackburn's contributions and paid tribute to the "father" of prison reforms in Kentucky. The Blackburn Correctional Complex, a 400-acre minimum-security prison near Lexington, is named for the commonwealth's "Good Samaritan" governor.

To the Blackburn family belonged several interesting and prominent men, including the governor's much younger brother, Joseph Clay Stiles Blackburn, a congressman from Kentucky for thirty-three years and later civilian governor of the Panama Canal Zone. This study, however, concentrates on Luke Blackburn's public career, to the exclusion of "Jo" Blackburn and others, for the absence of the doctor's private papers leaves unfortunate gaps in personal information about the physician and his relationships with members of his family.

Many persons aided in the collection of materials for this

study, and the author wishes to express her appreciation to them: the librarians at the Bermuda Library in Hamilton, the Mississippi Department of Archives and History at Jackson, the Louisiana State Museum in New Orleans, the Kentucky Historical Society and the Kentucky State Archives in Frankfort, the Frances Carrick Thomas Library at Transylvania University, the Margaret I. King Library at the University of Kentucky, the Filson Club in Louisville, and the Kentucky Library at Western Kentucky University.

Special thanks are extended to the editors of the *Filson Club History Quarterly*, the *Register of the Kentucky Historical Society*, and *Civil War Times, Illustrated* for their permission to use large portions of the author's articles published by them; to Western Kentucky University for a faculty grant that covered some of the research expenses involved in the study; to Professors Lowell H. Harrison and Carol Crowe-Carraco, who read the manuscript and made suggestions for its improvement; to my husband Tom, who served as medical consultant; and to my father, who needled me to "write a book about that character."

1

HEALTH OFFICER

O<small>N A RAINY</small> September evening in 1879, newly inaugurated Governor Luke Pryor Blackburn greeted constituents and visiting dignitaries who crowded into Frankfort's glittering Capitol Hotel ballroom to congratulate him. As he received their good wishes, the corpulent, white-haired governor must have reflected on the strange road that had brought him to this honor and responsibility. A native of Kentucky, he had spent most of his adult life in the Deep South, where he won acclaim as a health officer and humanitarian. What could a physician with little political experience contribute as the commonwealth's first citizen? Blackburn earlier had announced that he hoped to make improvements at the state's penitentiary, but most Kentuckians expected very little from the philanthropist. They saw his election as nothing more than a reward for the "Good Samaritan's" long devotion to victims of epidemic yellow fever and Asiatic cholera.

The Blackburns were among Kentucky's pioneer families. George and Prudence Blackburn, Luke's grandparents, came to Kentucky from Virginia about 1784 and built a log home and fort in the northern part of what became Woodford County. It was rumored that the Blackburns kept a pet bear at the fort, but whether the animal frightened away Indians or entertained the Blackburns' offspring is unknown. If the latter, the bruin had plenty of playmates, for the pioneer Blackburns raised at least twelve children to maturity. Luke's father, Edward M. ("Ned"), read law with George Nicholas and practiced his profession for many years, but he was best known as one of the state's leading breeders of fine horses. In 1809 Ned married fifteen-year-old Lavinia Bell and built for his rapidly increasing family a brick home, "Equira," at Spring Station. Luke, the fourth of their thirteen children, was born at sunrise on June 16, 1816.

Blackburn grew to maturity on the family's large Woodford County farm. Nothing is known about his formal schooling, but he undoubtedly derived much of his practical education from listening to the conversations of the men in his family. His maternal grandfather belonged to Kentucky's 1799 constitutional convention, his Blackburn grandfather hosted the famed Marquis de Lafayette during the general's Kentucky visit in 1825, and both grandfathers had known George Rogers Clark and other early explorers and settlers. Henry Clay was a distant cousin and an occasional visitor to the Blackburn home; Luke's Uncle William had served in the state legislature since 1808 and would be lieutenant governor during the administration of James T. Morehead; and a great-uncle, Gideon Blackburn, was the West's best-known Presbyterian minister, a former missionary to the Cherokee Indians, and a president of Centre College. Churchill Blackburn, another uncle, was an unusually well educated and highly esteemed physician in Paris, Kentucky. Medicine was the least prestigious of the professions in which the older Blackburns excelled, but it was the one that held the greatest attraction for young Luke. Shortly after his sixteenth birthday, he began a two-year apprenticeship with Churchill Blackburn and was engaged in this training when Asiatic cholera made its initial visit to Kentucky.

No Kentuckian, indeed no American, knew much about cholera in 1832. Medical books described it as an epidemic scourge of India and the Far East. Yet in 1828 it swept across Russia; the following year it decimated the German

2

states and by autumn of 1831 was ravaging the British Isles. In the spring of 1832 the pestilence crossed the Atlantic with immigrants, and throughout the summer it plagued North American port cities; 2,500 died in Montreal, 3,500 in New York City, 1,400 in Norfolk, 5,000 in New Orleans. On July 12 the *Lexington Observer and Reporter* predicted that the pestilence would reach every part of the United States.

Although most of her physicians had denied that the scourge would visit the commonwealth, cholera cases were reported in several Kentucky towns in the late fall of 1832. An early frost, however, ended the threat before the disease reached epidemic proportions. The death toll in Louisville was unofficially listed as 122. Maysville and Lexington each reported a few cases. A resident of the latter town wrote that the disease "killed five intemperates, frightened our citizens into strict temperance, drove away some of the faint hearted pupils [at Transylvania], and then took wing itself and troubled us no more."[1] Residents of the Bluegrass state breathed a premature sigh of relief.

Blackburn followed with concern the news of cholera's westward journey. He read in his uncle's medical books and in the various reports carried in the newspapers that cholera was believed to be a miasmatic disease, caused by poisonous gases produced by rotting vegetation and standing water. The malady, according to contemporary literature, was "excited" by the ingestion of green fruits and vegetables, by intemperance, and by strong emotion. Recommended treatments included bleeding, cupping, purging, and an infinite variety of medical concoctions.

In the summer of 1833 Blackburn gained firsthand knowledge of the disease when cholera hit the Bluegrass portion of Kentucky with vicious force. Maysville reported her first cholera deaths on May 29, and within thirty-six hours most of her white inhabitants had fled inland, carrying in their intestines the highly toxic *Vibrio comma*, the cholera-causing bacillus that is spread by careless disposal of sewage and subsequent contamination of the water supply. Most Kentuckians obtained water from poorly located wells that received frequent washings from shallow privies; in many parts of the state the springs that fed these wells ran through underground limestone caverns into which raw sewage was discharged. Thus, the disease hit areas with sudden, explosive force, affecting large portions of the population within a brief period.

The true cause of the scourge was unknown to Blackburn and other antebellum physicians, but they observed that cholera made a precipitous onset characterized by copious and purging diarrhea (and, eventually, "rice-water" stools), vomiting, subnormal temperatures, severe muscle cramps, and general prostration. Death generally occurred within thirty-six hours. For the small percentage who survived, recuperation was slow; immunity to future attacks would be temporary.

Cholera plagued most of the towns in central Kentucky in the summer of 1833, and residents experienced fright and hardships similar to those recorded in Lexington, where the malady raged unchecked throughout June and early July. Lexington, like most major towns, had a board of health whose contribution to the town's well-being was nebulous; during the epidemic the board members and other city officials fled and made no pretense of aiding the sick. Of Lexington's 6,000 residents, less than two-thirds remained in town; 500 of these died. A contemporary description of Lexington, previously labeled the state's healthiest town, sounds much like one of Europe during outbreaks of the bubonic plague.

The houses of business were all closed and scarcely anything was to be seen or heard in the streets except the hearse bearing its victims to the grave or some terrified messenger rushing or galloping for assistance. It was extremely difficult to have coffins and graves prepared in proper time for the dead. . . . If the pestilence here had any choice in its victims, it seemed to prefer the temperate and those who according to human reason were adjudged to be beyond its reach. The intemperate were generally spared—on the other hand some of our best citizens perished.[2]

Another Lexingtonian lamented that since "all the markets were suspended and the bakers' shops shut," there was "not a pound of beef to be got—and very little else. Not even a cracker for sale."[3]

Of the Lexington physicians in town throughout the entire epidemic, only Benjamin Dudley, a professor at Transylvania's medical department, survived without a sign of illness. At least seven of the town's practitioners died. Dr. Joseph Boswell, the father of Blackburn's future wife, became ill while making a house call in the country. Experiencing the sudden onset of abdominal cramps, he stopped at a farmhouse about six miles from Lexington and received permission to lie down on the porch. The lady of the house covered him with a blanket and went to fetch her husband; when she returned a few minutes later, Boswell was dead.

Late in June cholera struck Paris "with almost unparalleled malignity."[4] For three weeks Luke and his uncle aided the town's cholera victims, but despite their efforts and those of other doctors and volunteers, 10 percent of the town's population died. Nothing is known of Luke's specific deeds, but his thoughts were probably similar to those of a Danville apprentice who attended cholera patients and later wrote that he felt "terror and trembled like an inexperienced soldier who hears the report of the first gun that brings on the engagement," but "became courageous and met the destroyer [cholera] without faltering . . . [and] for the first time acted as a physician, giving medicine to those who requested my aid."[5] Certainly young Blackburn learned much about the psychological problems of a town under siege—of people waiting to be stricken by a mysterious malady and die, of the desperately ill who had no one to nurse them, of small children trying to care for their sick parents, of orphans who became public charity cases, or uncoffined bodies, shallow, mass graves, lack of food, lack of everything. It was a lesson he would never forget.

Upon completion of his two-year apprenticeship, a nineteenth-century form of premedical training, seventeen-year-old Blackburn entered the medical department of Transylvania University, one of the nation's oldest and most prestigious schools. As at other medical institutions of the antebellum period, Transylvania's academic year extended from November 1 to February 28. Graduation requirements included attendance at two of the annual sessions, satisfactory passage of a comprehensive oral examination, and the completion of a thesis.

Blackburn's eighteen-page thesis, entitled "Cholera Maligna," reiterated most of the accepted theories of the day. He noted that the disease was fickle in its selection of sites and victims, but that it had an affinity for watercourses, and it struck "like a thunderstorm or whirlwind." Cholera was more likely to be fatal to those whose constitutions were weakened by intemperance or impoverished diets than to the healthy, Blackburn wrote, and it was caused by eating crude vegetables or unripe fruits and drinking acid beverages, beer, porter, and "bad water," an inclusion he did not explain. Blackburn had learned that during the Lexington epidemic all residents of the town, even those not stricken by cholera, suffered from disorders of the gastrointestinal system; "the epidemic principle bears a specific relation to the alimentary mucous surface . . . impairing its function." The young man concluded that the effect of cholera on the body was that of a "universal sedation of organic life, manifested in the capillary tissue, then in the larger vessels and heart," thus causing bodily functions to cease.[6]

Blackburn received his medical degree in March 1835, three months before his nineteenth birthday, and opened an office on Lexington's Main Street, where he and an associate "gratuitously prescribe for the poor every day at 7 A.M."[7] The partnership was brief. Cholera struck Versailles in August, and the local physicians either fled from the disease or became victims of it. Hearing of the town's plight, Blackburn went to Versailles, and he and at least one other doctor worked day and night to care for the sick. A resident of the town later labeled Blackburn the "kindest and most gentle yet bravest man" he ever met, for he "entered homes of the sick and dying, and many did he bring back from the jaws of death by his skill and intrepid nerve."[8] Nineteenth-century accounts indicate that Blackburn remained in Versailles at the cessation of the epidemic because of pleas from local residents that he do so, but his family ties with the area undoubtedly influenced his decision also.

In November of 1835 Luke married his distant cousin, Ella Gist Boswell, one of the many orphans of the 1833 Lexington epidemic. Ella's ancestors were also early explorers and settlers from Virginia. Her father, a former army surgeon, had practiced medicine in Lexington for nearly three decades and had been part-owner of several of that town's mercantile establishments. An older brother was known for his fine racehorses.

Little is known of the Blackburns' life in Versailles. The practice of medicine, especially in rural areas, was generally not lucrative, and Blackburn's income may have been insufficient for his growing family. Shortly before the 1837 birth of his only son, Cary Bell, the doctor invested his savings in a company that manufactured hemp products. Unfortunately the enterprise failed, and Blackburn suffered a considerable loss. In 1843 he campaigned as the Whig candidate from Woodford County and was elected to the Kentucky House of Representatives, but he served without distinction and apparently was not interested in a second term. A year later the Blackburns moved to Frankfort where Luke and a younger brother shared an office on Saint Claire Street. Their advertisement promised that a servant would always be present to aid ladies in and out of carriages and to return home those patients who were too ill to travel alone.

Flush times in Mississippi during the 1840s attracted many Kentuckians, including the Blackburns. In the early months of 1846 the doctor and his family moved to Natchez, a town famous for its wealthy elegance, brawling riverfront, and fine racetrack. The Boswells and Blackburns were well known to Natchez residents. Ella's brother frequently raced his prize-winning horses there, and some of the area's best horses and cattle had been born on Ned

Blackburn's Woodford County farm. The Blackburns purchased a home on Canewood Place, next door to the Presbyterian parsonage, and Ella was delighted with the interest the doctor exhibited in its furnishings and yard plantings. Cary briefly attended the Natchez Institute, one of the South's early public schools, but in the fall of 1848 he returned to Kentucky to stay with his grandparents and study with Mr. B. B. Sayre at the Frankfort Academy. Ella sorely missed the absent child, who was "never out of my mind." Moreover, she wrote, "I had no idea that Doctor would take being separated from him so hard, still he says he knows it is best for the child's own good."[9]

In Natchez Blackburn quickly became active in community affairs. The doctor served as his father's agent for residents who wished to purchase Kentucky cattle; he helped found a temperance society and was elected honorary captain of the Natchez Fencibles, an elite militia group. When the town honored Jefferson Davis and the First Regiment of Mississippi Volunteers returning from the war with Mexico, Blackburn served on the planning committee and as toastmaster at the "heart inspiring" reception for the "laureled volunteers." The troops, conducted from the wharf to the promenade grounds by various city militia groups, were presented with bouquets from students at the Natchez Institute and enjoyed a "sumptuously loaded board" prepared by the women of Natchez. Toasts led by Blackburn "sped merrily around the board" as hosts and guests saluted the nation, the president, Major Generals Zachary Taylor and Winfield Scott, "Old Kentucky," the First Mississippi Regiment, and the ladies, the "first to cheer the soldiers on—the first to welcome them back."[10]

Blackburn's circle of friends in Natchez included Davis and other social and political figures of the area, but William Johnson, the famed "barber of Natchez," was his most interesting acquaintance. A free Negro and a slave owner, Johnson kept a diary which he filled with business transactions, family news, and local gossip. Included in it were notations of Blackburn's visits to ailing members of Johnson's

8

family, services the barber rendered for Blackburn, and the death notice of one of the doctor's brothers, killed during a street brawl in Frankfort. The diary also contained Blackburn's annual bill for professional services—one dollar for each office call and two dollars for each house call, regardless of the malady treated. In 1851 Johnson died from a gunshot wound inflicted by a neighbor with whom he had quarreled over a boundary question. In his dying breath the barber named his assassin to Blackburn and heard the doctor promise to care for his friend's family. Blackburn served as one of the executors for Johnson's estate and for many years, even after he moved from Mississippi, acted as an advisor to Johnson's widow and many children.

During his Natchez years Luke enjoyed a lucrative career. In November 1853 he informed his father that he had netted $10,000 that year from the practice of medicine, a handsome income even for an area where the cost of living was outrageously high. Ella hoped that they could save enough money to buy a farm in Kentucky and return there to spend "the rest of our days in comfort." Although she was homesick for the Bluegrass state, Ella admitted that she had never seen her husband "as happy and contented as he is now. . . . rich, poor, high, low respect him. No one can say a word against him, and it is quite a by-word in town to be as temperate as Dr. B." To his mother Blackburn revealed the key to his professional success: "I attend to my business closely and beat everyone with courtesy."[11]

Blackburn's office was in his home, but his practice was not limited to office patients. Shortly after his arrival in Natchez he arranged with the town officials to assume the management of the city hospital. In preparation for his new responsibility as administrator and medical consultant, Blackburn studied facilities in New Orleans and found both the city and its hospitals "disagreeable, dull, dirty places." The Natchez hospital, he decided, would be "conducted very differently." Blackburn hired his brother Henry and another young doctor to act as resident physicians and provide constant medical and nursing care; a family servant also lived at the hospital and kept it and the grounds "immaculately clean." A large portion of the hospital's patients were "servants of different plantations" whose masters paid one dollar per day for their care. "Owners find it much cheaper to send them to the hospital than to employ a physician to see them," Ella told her in-laws, for "doctor's fees in this country are very high . . . two dollars in town, one dollar more to write a prescription. . . . when they are called in the country it is a dollar per mile."[12]

Blackburn's hospital also cared for charity patients, and a large percentage of these were rivermen who sickened en route from New Orleans or Memphis. Although his hospital filled the need, Blackburn believed that the state or federal government should provide the service, and he urged Mississippi Congressman Albert G. Brown to appeal for funds for a government-supported facility at Natchez. The creation of "marine" hospitals had been discussed in the national legislature on several occasions, but no action resulted. Brown appeared before a naval appropriations committee, told of the Natchez doctor who used his own funds to provide hospital care for the sick rivermen, and chided Congress for not creating accommodations for the nation's inland sailors. In the Senate, Brown's plea was echoed by an Arkansas medic, Solon Borland, who informed his fellow senators that despite millions in revenue collected from western commerce, boatmen were "dependent on the charity of the towns for means to pay for medicine" and on local physicians for medical care.[13] In February 1849 Congress appropriated $60,000 for six marine hospitals along the Mississippi. When the facility at Natchez was completed in the spring of 1852, Blackburn was named its chief physician and surgeon. Shortly after accepting the marine hospital directorship, he resigned from his duties at the city hospital and opened a small infirmary exclusively for blacks. The facility accepted any medical problem except smallpox, and medical and nursing care and "surgical operations of whatever description" were made available for one dollar per day, but no patient was refused because of insufficient funds.[14] Nothing more is known of Blackburn's efforts in behalf of the rivermen and blacks, but his activities received praise from his contemporaries.

Although many of the diseases treated by Blackburn in private practice and at his hospitals were those he had seen in Kentucky, in Natchez he was introduced to another of the world's great plagues—yellow fever. During the colonial and early federal period this viral disease killed thousands in urban areas along the East Coast, but after 1825 its most vicious attacks were in the Deep South, especially in the Mississippi Valley. Transported from the West Indies to New Orleans and other gulf ports, yellow fever was usually present, and when conditions were right it flared into frightening epidemics, depopulating urban areas, paralyzing trade and industry, and keeping southerners in a state of perpetual dread. The cause of the disease was unknown until 1900, when Dr. Walter Reed discovered that the female *Aëdes aegypti* mosquito (which is native to a large portion of the United States) acted as a vector host and transmitted the disease from person to person. Yellow fever was carried upriver by sick refugees fleeing from fever-ridden areas, and the severity and northward extension of its nearly annual appearance depended on how early in the season the disease appeared in the gulf area, how great was the concentration of mosquitoes and of susceptible persons, and when the first autumnal frost killed the insects.

The mortality rate from yellow fever was 30 to 50 percent, for no cure was known. A few days after being bitten by an infected mosquito, victims of the disease experienced increasingly severe headache and backache, high fever, and extreme nausea; signs of impending death included "black vomit" (caused by hemorrhaging mucous membranes) and jaundice (a symptom of liver cell destruction). Those who survived the lengthy convalescence enjoyed a lifelong immunity to the disease. Since most of its victims were newcomers to the South, yellow fever was often called the "stranger's disease."

Natchez, surrounded by swamps where mosquitoes bred,

had a well-deserved reputation as an unhealthy town. A board of health consisting of five appointed laymen and an elected physician-health officer attempted to supervise the area's health. Accepting the two major contemporary theories that miasma or fomites (clothing or other objects that harbor pathogens) transmitted yellow fever, the board had long urged residents to drain water-filled sinkholes, cover cisterns and wells, and disinfect privies. During threatened fever epidemics they made half-hearted attempts to prevent riverboats with illness aboard from docking at the city wharf and to set up quarantine stations below Natchez to accommodate sick refugees. Unfortunately, the board lacked any means to enforce its regulations. Businessmen discouraged the enactment of stringent quarantines and refused to abide by the measures that were suggested. A quarantine hampered commerce.

In 1848 Blackburn was elected Natchez's health officer, and that summer when yellow fever began its deadly journey up the river, Blackburn persuaded the board of health to establish a quarantine station below the city. All Natchez-bound persons from infected areas remained at the station for twenty-four hours to "allow the yellow fever to escape from their person." Entry of sick persons into the city was forbidden.[15] Blackburn also urged residents to clean and disinfect their property and to eliminate all standing water, rotting vegetation, and other sources of miasma. Although neighboring towns were severely stricken, Natchez apparently remained relatively free from the disease. William Johnson wrote in his diary that there were "some reports of Fever," especially "Billous fever," and noted that the town's residents were "devided in the oppinion about the Disease." Local officials maintained that Natchez was healthy, and in a typical gesture intended to aid the town's trade and calm its frightened residents, the local press repeatedly invited refugees to seek safety in Natchez, "as healthy a place as there is on earth."[16] Whatever the fever rate, it was not epidemic. In praising Blackburn's efforts the *Natchez Daily Courier* revealed that the town's good health had been purchased at a relatively minor expense—$1,959 for the quarantine station and various supplies needed for the ill as compared to $4,000 spent by the city during the 1843 epidemic for "sanitary purposes."[17]

Between 1849 and 1853 cholera and yellow fever were sporadic in Natchez. "This poor southern country is doomed all summer and fall. . . . We never know when we are safe," Ella complained to her mother-in-law in Kentucky.[18] In the summer of 1853 epidemic yellow fever again raged along the Mississippi River. Before the pestilence reached Natchez, Blackburn urged the town's new health officer and board of health to institute protective measures, but the merchants who controlled the board refused to consider his suggestions. Their stubborn attitude was costly. Many of the town's residents fled as the disease approached the city, and several store owners moved their businesses to inland towns, but among those remaining were hundreds of "Yellow Jack's" victims. The Blackburns' neighbor wrote that during the scourge's four-month visit "the places of business were generally closed, the grass literally sprung up in our untrodden streets; and the silence, not of a Sabbath but of the funeral hour, hung over our usually bustling city."[19] Four hundred and fifty of the town's five thousand residents died during the epidemic, and more than $9,000 in public and private funds were expended on provisions for the ill and orphaned.

During the 1853 epidemic Blackburn attended the sick day and night and kept in readiness "two pairs of buggy horses, besides a pair of carriage horses and his riding horse." Ella, immune to the disease after a light case of it several years earlier, worried about her "beloved husband slaving himself" and feared he would contract the disease. At the end of the epidemic she expressed her hatred for the fever-ridden town. "If all the wealth in the world was offered to me for me to stay and undergo what I did this summer, I would not accept it. The anxiety of mind was itself enough to wear anyone out. I was in Lexington in 1832 [1833] when the cholera first made its appearance but it was not to be compared to what I have witnessed this summer." They hoped, she told Luke's mother, to return to Kentucky in two or three years, purchase a farm, and "pass the rest of . . . [our] lives in safety, surrounded by all we hold dear. This is not a place to raise a boy."[20]

If the 1853 epidemic was a frightening ordeal for Ella, it was professionally educational for her husband. During the epidemic Blackburn observed various treatments used by Natchez doctors and compiled a relatively large number of statistics. He concluded from them that those patients given little or no medication were more likely to survive an attack of the malady than were the ones physicians overdosed with quinine (a standard remedy for malaria, a disease many physicians believed related to yellow fever), and other noxious agents. Liquids (especially warm lemonade), ice (generally considered dangerous for patients suffering from high fever), sweating, foot baths, and "blistering" (drawing out "disease-producing poisons" by creating a blister with a hot object) if "black vomit" appeared, were Blackburn's favorite remedies. The use of ice, which reduced fever, and the replacement of body fluids, preventing dehydration, probably were the most effective remedies available during the nineteenth century.

When the scourge began its northward march the following summer, Blackburn was drafted as the town's health officer, and, despite protests, he rigidly enforced a quarantine. All persons from ravaged areas were now required to spend two weeks at the station—one week would have sufficed—before entering the city, and vessels from stricken areas were forbidden to dock. Sick refugees received care at the station hospital. Blackburn also convinced the frightened town officials that they should pass an ordinance directing physicians to report suspected cases of yellow fever to him, and he personally investigated every case. The Natchez press constantly assured its readers that the city was experiencing a healthier season than it had known in years and praised Blackburn as an excellent public servant. Despite loud complaints voiced by some local businessmen, the

14

quarantine remained in effect until late October, when, according to the press, it was "too late for yellow fever to originate from atmospheric causes."[21] Blackburn's efforts had produced the first effective quarantine ever used in the Mississippi Valley.

In his report to the board of health in late October, the doctor emphasized that the use of the quarantine had been tested and proved effective, for Natchez remained healthy while all other towns below Memphis were visited by the fever. Natchez should use the quarantine, Blackburn admonished, whenever it became necessary to protect her residents.

With the lifting of the quarantine Blackburn resigned his post. At his last meeting with the board on October 21, he informed the city officials that he had fought against much opposition, but had that opposition been "tenfold greater, I should not have been deterred." However, he added, "Nothing could tempt me again to solicit or accept this responsible yet thankless office."[22] The city council voted to pay the doctor $200, twice the health officer's annual salary, for his services during the summer. When he refused to accept any compensation, the residents of the area expressed their gratitude with a gift of twin silver pitchers and trays that were appropriately engraved.

Having prevented yellow fever from striking his home area, Blackburn encouraged Louisiana to erect a quarantine station below New Orleans that would protect the entire valley. In a letter to the New Orleans Sanitary Commission on Epidemic Yellow Fever, Blackburn stressed that "quarantine may be better enforced in New Orleans than anywhere on the Mississippi river and without an efficient quarantine *there*, our quarantines on the river, unless of a most expensive and inquisitorial character (guarding every road and approach to town) cannot be considered perfect." As to opposition raised because a quarantine hurt commerce, Blackburn warned that to "put trade against human life would call down the indignation of the humane and civilized world and it would be best rebuked by a visit to the

Pitcher and tray presented to Blackburn
by the people of Adams County, Mississippi.
Courtesy of Kentucky Historical Society

populous cemeteries of your city, where hecatombs from every region of our country, as well as your native town, sleep the sleep that knows no awakening; victims to the unobstructed admission of yellow fever from its home in the tropics."[23]

In January 1855, when the Southern Commercial Convention met in New Orleans, Blackburn addressed its committee on quarantine. The convention approved a resolution supporting quarantine stations along the Gulf of Mexico and presented it to the Louisiana legislature, which was then debating the advisability of establishing a station below the Crescent City. Blackburn also made a personal appeal to the Louisiana lawmakers and aided them in drawing up an "Act to establish quarantine for the protection of the state." The law, approved in March 1855, provided for quarantine stations at the mouths of the state's major rivers. These stations were to be administered by the State Board of Health, the nation's first permanent state body established to protect and promote public health. Although the regulations included in the act should have been adequate to prevent the introduction of foreign maladies, opposition from commercial interests soon hampered their effective administration. Yellow fever and cholera continued to plague the Mississippi Valley.

Yellow Jack and cholera were only two of the Deep South's fatal diseases; malaria, typhoid, and a host of other endemic maladies constantly threatened life and health. In November of 1856 Ella Blackburn, who suffered chronically from dropsy and a nervous condition, died from one of the illnesses indigenous to the Natchez area. The September before her demise Blackburn and their eighteen-year-old son Cary had traveled to Philadelphia, where Cary began an apprenticeship with the eminent Dr. Samuel David Gross in anticipation of his entrance to one of the medical schools in Philadelphia. While in the East, Blackburn answered a call for help issued by Long Island officials when an outbreak of yellow fever threatened to engulf the metropolitan area. Frightened residents of the area had stormed a temporary fever hospital erected by the port authority, for they recalled tales of the terrible 1793 epidemic in Philadelphia and feared the spread of contagion from the hospital. While officials on the island and the port authority calmed the panic-stricken residents, Blackburn and other physicians cared for scores of fever victims. No records were kept, but the death count was estimated at 160.

When he returned to Natchez the doctor found his frail wife suffering from the effects of a "fever." Despite his ministrations, her strength ebbed away. The loss of his wife and the distance between him and his family and child plunged the physician into a deep grief that worried his friends. They urged him to get away from Natchez, to take the European trip he had long talked about but never had time to make.

Blackburn sailed for the continent in the spring of 1857 to study Europe's hospitals. His friends wrote letters of introduction to their European friends and described Blackburn as a "gentleman of the highest standing socially and professionally" who had "ample stores of worldly goods" and had been "crowned with honors . . . by the elite of Natchez."[24] Nothing is known of Blackburn's itinerary except that he visited in Rome and Paris. Apparently the sea air and his brief rambles through Old World hospitals dispelled his grief, for in Paris he was smitten by charming, vivacious, twenty-four-year-old Julia Churchill, the youngest daughter of Samuel and Abigail Churchill of Louisville. Julia had been traveling for several months with her sister, Emily Zane, and Emily's consumptive ten-year-old daughter, Abby. The Kentuckians cut short their travels and returned to the United States in the early fall to talk with Julia's parents. In November 1857 Luke and Julia were married in a formal ceremony at the bride's home and then left for a honeymoon in the South.

Julia's grace and warmth charmed Blackburn's Natchez friends, who hoped that the blue-eyed bride and their favorite doctor would remain in the river town, but in January of 1858 the couple decided to make their home in New Orleans. Shortly after their move Cary joined his father in the small medical office on Saint Charles and Canal streets.

The Blackburns were sorely missed by their relatives in Louisville and friends in Natchez, but they made frequent trips to both towns and welcomed visits to New Orleans from their kin and former neighbors. Frail little Abby was one of their favorite guests. Between her twice-yearly visits to their home, Abby's letters kept them abreast of the latest family news—of a cousin suffering from the "New York mallidy [*sic*] of nothing to wear," of the elderly widower Samuel Churchill "getting quite gay . . . he gave a dinner Party a week or so ago and invited his eastern neighbors and night before last he gave a bird supper and invited them again," and of the new icehouse Abby's father was building so that they could provide the doctor with "as much pound cake and ice cream when you come up next summer as you can eat."[25] The Blackburns were visiting in Louisville in the spring of 1860 when death released Abby from the pain she had suffered with tuberculosis.

Julia's only child, also named Abby, briefly brightened their lives. Tucked among the few items Julia preserved is an undated poem, in the doctor's handwriting, entitled "Lines for my little wife Julia, To her first born Abby."

> *I've a wee thing to love, an infant new born*
> *With cheeks like a rose and breath fresh as the morn*
> *And we thought when she first op'd her bright, beaming eyes*
> *That twin stars had fallen in my bed from the skies. . . .*[26]

The infant's birth and death dates are unknown; the poem is the only record of the baby's existence. Nevertheless, it reveals the tender side of the man accused of authoring one of the most sinister schemes of the Civil War.

2

CONFEDERATE AGENT

IN THE DECADE before the outbreak of the Civil War, many of Luke's and Julia's brothers had moved from Kentucky to Illinois, Missouri, Arkansas, Mississippi, and Louisiana. Within a few months after hostilities began in the spring of 1861, all of them, even those living in Union states, joined the Confederate army. Although he was a states' rightist and a slave owner, Luke was the families' exception. His reluctance to enlist may have been due to his age (forty-five) and lack of military experience, but why the doctor did not volunteer his desperately needed skills to the Confederate medical department is unknown. Instead of choosing the more obvious way to serve the South, Blackburn selected the peculiar role of civilian agent.

Information about Blackburn's activities during the first two years of the war is sketchy. He served as an unsuccessful envoy for Governor Beriah Magoffin of Kentucky to obtain guns from Louisiana for the defense of the commonwealth, and early in 1862 he joined the forces of Sterling Price in Mississippi as the general's civilian aide-de-camp. For several months Blackburn traveled around the South, delivering messages concerning troop movements and securing arms for Price's poorly supplied army. By late August he had obtained 8,000 guns, which he took to Columbia, Mississippi, and Gainesville, Alabama, for repairs. When he informed Price of his acquisition, Blackburn also announced that

30,000 additional arms had just arrived at one of the southern ports. "You will get your portion," he promised.[1]

In February of 1863 Mississippi Governor John J. Pettus appointed two commissioners "to get all of Mississippi's invalid soldiers together in one ward or hospital so that their wants may be attended to without so much loss or inconvenience in the transportation of articles sent to them."[2] Blackburn was one of the commissioners, and throughout the late winter and spring he visited military hospitals in Mississippi and Alabama. Unable to secure one facility large enough to care for all the sick and wounded, he established several accommodations for convalescents. Upon completing his assignment, the doctor visited Richmond and offered his services to the secretary of war as "General Inspector of Hospitals and Camps. . . . I am willing to take this position without pay or rank." Recommendations from the "entire delegation" to the Confederate Congress from Kentucky, Mississippi, Arkansas, and Tennessee accompanied the application.[3] When the doctor's offer was refused, he wrote to the commander at Mobile that he would like to work with the blockade runners. Blackburn proposed to purchase or lease a seagoing vessel from the northern lakes ("but not from Yankees"), load it with ice and other desperately needed commodities, and run it through the blockade to Mobile.[4] In exchange for Confederate protection at the gulf port, the doctor would give the Confederates most of the ice, selling just enough to cover his expenses, and then reload the vessel with cotton and ship it to Havana. The plan was approved, and Pettus appointed Blackburn as Mississippi's agent in Canada to gather supplies for blockade runners. The doctor remained in Mississippi throughout the summer, aiding soldiers wounded during the siege of Vicksburg. In late August of 1863 he and his wife sailed for Halifax and then traveled on to Toronto, where they took rooms at a boardinghouse operated by a Mr. Withers from Covington.

Julia, who had been with her family in Louisville since the summer of 1862, had to obtain special permission to cross Federal lines into the South to join her Canada-bound husband. Permission was granted, but she was informed that she could take only one trunk of personal belongings and no more than $1,000 in cash. Should she return to Federal territory before the war's end, she was admonished, she would be "considered a spy" and treated as such.[5]

Shortly after they arrived in Canada, Blackburn obtained a ship and filled it with ice and other items. On his arrival at Mobile, Pettus ordered that the doctor be given fifty bales of cotton to exchange in Cuba for arms, ammunition, and money. But a Federal patrol boat captured the small vessel as it attempted to leave the harbor, and the ship and its cargo were impounded. The Federals assumed that the doctor was a civilian passenger, for he was released and allowed to return to Upper Canada. There, he began to contemplate using his medical knowledge to slay the enemy.

During his days in Mississippi, Blackburn and several of his associates had relieved their fatigue and raised their spirits with empty talk in which they tried to outdo each other with plans that would assure the Yankees' defeat. Blackburn jokingly suggested that yellow fever caused more deaths than any army could; perhaps the South needed Bronze John to lead her to victory. The more he thought of the idea, the more it seemed a real possibility for saving the South. Infected clothing imported into northern cities might trigger an epidemic severe enough to halt the Union's war machine, Blackburn reasoned. It was a diabolical scheme, but perhaps the doctor had patched up enough mangled southern bodies to adopt the thinking of his brother James, who wrote after his initiation on the battlefield: "From this day I hold every *Union traitor* as my enemy. . . . I intend to begin the work of murder in earnest, and if I ever spare one of them may hell be my portion. I want to see Union blood flow deep enough for my horse to swim in."[6] It is possible that during his travels in the South, Blackburn approached officials in Richmond with his plan. If so, they probably did not approve it, but neither did they forbid him to use germ warfare against the enemy.

Other southerners also were cognizant of the havoc that yellow fever could visit on the Union army. Although a few creole rebels refused to believe that a merciful God would send the pestilence and the Yankees to plague them at the same time, many residents of Union-occupied New Orleans hoped that "his saffron Majesty" would make his annual visit to the city and "wave his sceptre" over the unwelcome intruders. Union soldiers stationed in the Crescent City had heard of the fever's preference for newcomers, especially northerners, and New Orleanians of all ages took advantage of the oppressors' fear. Children harassed the men in blue by chanting

> *Yellow Jack will grab them up*
> *And take them all away,*

and adults hinted that their silent prayers at church were for the disease to come "as a divine interposition." More daring than wise, two pranksters intensified the fear when they walked up to a group of Federals and checked their heights with a tape measure. Recording the measurements in a notebook, they informed the soldiers that they had received a contract to supply ten thousand coffins to the army for expected fever victims. Under the barrage of demoralizing propaganda, army officials were understandably deluged with desertions, requests for transfers, and cases of severe depression.[7]

General Benjamin Butler, commander of the occupational forces in New Orleans from April to November of 1862, was determined to protect his troops. After talking with local physicians and studying contemporary literature relating to yellow fever, Butler instituted a program that combined the two major protective devices long suggested by the South's physicians—quarantine and sanitation. All ships entering the Mississippi River were stopped and inspected at Fort Saint Philip near the river's mouth. If given a clean bill-of-health by the health inspector, the boat proceeded upriver to the city. Those vessels with sickness aboard and all ships that had touched fever-infested ports were required to spend forty days at the quarantine station seventy-five miles below the city. Butler armed the station and ordered that any vessel attempting to pass it without permission was to be fired upon. The health officer at Fort Saint Philip was well paid for his duties but was threatened with the death penalty if he allowed an infected ship to reach the city.

Assured that the disease could not be imported, Butler began the Augean task of cleaning New Orleans of more than a century of filth. A force of 2,000 men "fully provided with the necessary tools and supervision" and "accompanied by a few bayonets," scraped and scrubbed the filth-laden streets and drains; thereafter the city waterworks flushed them periodically to keep them free of debris. Every householder was required to cleanse his property inside and out, and anyone who refused to obey Butler's sanitation regulations was arrested and taken to jail. Thus Butler cleaned the city that previously "cultivated a condition of perfect nastiness," and his successor maintained the high degree of cleanliness achieved through "Beast Butler's" military despotism.[8] The enforced regulations and Union naval blockade were largely responsible for the unusual good health enjoyed by New Orleans during the war years.

Although the Crescent City remained free of the disease, yellow fever plagued the West Indies. In the spring of 1864, shortly after the malady broke out in Bermuda, Blackburn slipped quietly out of Halifax and went to the islands to help physicians there care for fever victims. In mid-July he returned to Halifax with eight trunks, five of which, it was later alleged, contained linens and clothing from the beds of his Bermuda patients. He had previously arranged to be met by J. W. Harris, an alias for Godfrey J. Hyams, whom he enlisted to take the trunks to northern cities and sell their contents to used-clothing merchants. When the cargo was aboard a steamer for Boston, Blackburn returned to Toronto.

By late August of 1864 the fever epidemic in Bermuda was so severe it threatened to paralyze blockade-running activities between the island and southern coastal cities. Blackburn volunteered his services to the Bermuda government and again sailed for the islands, arriving about September 4. During his second visit he resided at the Hamilton Hotel in Saint George and cared for hundreds of fever victims. His activities were closely watched by the American consul, Charles M. Allen, who discovered that Blackburn "refused all offers of a pecuniary nature, either for his services here or for expenses incurred by his visit, claiming to have had much experience in the treatment of this disease and being desirous only of benefiting this community, who had manifested so much sympathy for their 'Holy Cause.' " Allen also noted that the doctor "never neglected to advertise on all possible occasions the cause of the rebels."[9]

Blackburn remained in Bermuda until the epidemic abated in mid-October. During his ministrations to the ill he filled several trunks with soiled clothing and linens, and before his departure from the island he attempted to find someone who would smuggle the goods into northern cities the following spring. He approached a well-known blockade runner who periodically docked at Union ports, and told him of his plan. Shocked by the cold-bloodedness of the doctor's scheme, the boatman "shouted, not in the choicest of language, to leave the office."[10] Blackburn finally found a resident of Saint George, Edward Swan, who agreed to store the trunks until the doctor could return to claim them or could make arrangements for their removal to Halifax. Details completed, Blackburn sailed for Canada. A few weeks thereafter the Queen's Admiralty announced that a gift of £100, a token of their appreciation, would be presented to Blackburn for his philanthropic work in Bermuda.

Blackburn's activities during the remaining months of the war are a mystery, but it is likely that he was involved in more than one of the various schemes concocted by his Confederate associates in Canada, who tried to take advantage of discontentment among residents of Union states, create panic among northern city dwellers, and force civilians in Union states to experience some of the horrors of war. Several of these agents were Kentuckians whose friendships Blackburn would value throughout his life—the Reverend Stuart Robinson, a Louisville Presbyterian minister who had studied with Gideon Blackburn; Thomas Hines, John B. Castleman, and Bennett Young, former raiders with John Hunt Morgan; and John Headley. Hines authored an elaborate plan to set off a massive insurrection in the northwest and burn several northern cities to draw attention from the Chicago area, where he and local Copperheads (antiwar and pro-Confederate residents of the North) would aid the escape of military prisoners at Chicago's Camp Douglas. Blackburn was to lead diversionary forces against Boston. An inebriated rebel prisoner revealed the plan, and troops were moved into Boston, thus thwarting Blackburn's part of the scheme. Hines, who expected to lead the prison break, owed his escape from Federal authorities in Chicago to Mary Morris, Blackburn's sister, who was married to a local judge.

As the various Confederate armies surrendered during the weeks following Appomattox, the Blackburns probably made plans for their eventual return to the South. Warrants had been issued in the United States for the arrest of several of his Confederate friends in Canada, but the doctor's name had not been linked to their activities. As far as Union officials knew, he was merely a civilian living in Toronto. Then, in late April of 1865, Blackburn's world exploded.

On the same day President Lincoln was assassinated, Consul Charles Allen in Bermuda wired details of a newly discovered plot to authorities in Washington. He had just learned from a rebel agent that the "sole object" of Blackburn's visit the previous autumn had been to collect fever patients' contaminated clothing, which he planned to send to New York and other northern cities during the coming summer. Three of the trunks, Allen understood, remained in the care of a man in Blackburn's employ, Edward Swan, who was to ship them to Halifax, Nova Scotia, in June. The trunks were confiscated, taken to the local quarantine station, and found to contain bundles of clean wearing apparel and bedding wrapped with "dirty flannel drawers and shirts . . . evidently taken from a sick bed." Tucked among them were "some poultices and many other things which could have been placed there for no legitimate purpose." The local health officer saturated the trunks and their contents with sulfuric acid and buried them.[11]

On receipt of Allen's information the Department of State informed Judge Advocate General Joseph Holt, then preparing for the trial of President Lincoln's assassins, of the recently discovered plot, and the Bureau of Military Justice ordered the arrest of Dr. Blackburn for murder. The physician was in Canada and beyond the jurisdiction of the United States, but in a too eager attempt to produce immediate results, the Saint Louis police mistakenly arrested an Indian herbal doctor named Francis Tumblety, alias J. H. Blackburn. Taken to Washington and held for three weeks in the Old Capitol Prison, Tumblety was then released without a hearing or an apology.

Edward Swan was also arrested and appeared before the Saint George magistrates in Bermuda for a hearing. The Saint George health officer testified that he had examined a green trunk, a black trunk, and a small leather portmanteau taken from Swan's home. In them he found articles bearing dark stains that resembled those made by "black vomit." Swan told the magistrates that Blackburn had promised to pay him $150 for storing the trunks. A nurse informed them that she helped Blackburn take numerous woolen shirts from a large green trunk, and cover his patients with them to aid "sweating"; then she saw the doctor repack the shirts in the trunk. Another witness, who had earlier accused a servant of the theft, commented on the strange disappearance of the soiled bed linens on which one of Blackburn's patients died. The barkeeper at the hotel where Blackburn stayed swore that the doctor arrived at the hotel with only one trunk but returned to Halifax with two or three trunks and left instructions that several others should be sent to the home of Mr. Swan. A cart driver told the magistrates that he took several pieces of baggage to Swan's home, and another man revealed that Blackburn inquired of him about Swan's honesty, saying he planned to pay Swan $250 to store several trunks. Sufficient evidence of Swan's activities was presented to warrant a trial. Swan was remanded to the jail until his appearance before the Court of General Assizes, which found him "guilty of being a nuisance" and sentenced him to four months in prison.[12]

The *New York Times* and other northern newspapers copied reports of the sensational trial from Bermuda papers. The front page stories, which were soon overshadowed by articles about the Lincoln assassination hearing and the capture of Confederate President Jefferson Davis, contained embellishments and fabrications. Financial backing for the plot reportedly came from a variety of sources—the Confederate government, rebel sympathizers in Havana, and the sale of cotton provided by the governor of Mississippi. Blackburn was described as an ultrarebel, a vindictive traitor, and a quack-physician from Kentucky, Mississippi, or Louisiana. The *New York Times* speculated that the physician might have been involved in the slave trade, for the paper believed he was a co-owner of the slave ship, *Wanderer*. No mention was made of Blackburn's prewar medical activities.

A few days after Americans first heard of the yellow fever plot, the story was greatly enhanced with sensational revelations given in Detroit by Godfrey J. Hyams, alias J. H. Harris, a Union informer who earlier had sold names of known Copperheads to Union officials and had testified against several rebel agents, including Kentuckian Bennett Young. Hyams claimed that he acted as Blackburn's agent in July of 1864 and took trunks of infected clothing from Halifax to Boston, Philadelphia, Washington, and Norfolk, where he sold them to used clothing merchants. On May 19 the Canadian authorities arrested Blackburn in Montreal, charged him with conspiracy to commit murder, took him to Toronto, and examined him before the Toronto Police Court. The hearing generated interest among local residents, and the courtroom was crowded with spectators.

Hyams, the first witness to appear against Blackburn, claimed to have known the physician in Arkansas but said they were formally introduced by Stuart Robinson at the Queen's Hotel of Toronto in December 1863. Believing that Hyams wanted to serve the South, the doctor had offered him a job that would do "more good for the Confederate cause than if I were to bring 100,000 men to reinforce Lee; [he promised] that I would come to have more honor and glory to my name than the General had." Blackburn had explained his scheme to Hyams and promised to pay him $60,000 when the job was successfully completed.[13]

His next contact with Blackburn, Hyams related, was six months later when he received a letter from the physician, written on May 10 from Bermuda, asking him to borrow the necessary travel money and meet with him in Halifax as soon as possible. After some difficulty in obtaining the funds from various Confederates in Toronto and Montreal, Hyams reached Halifax in late June. On July 18 Blackburn arrived aboard the mailboat *Alpha* with eight trunks and a valise, which Hyams and the ship's officer, W. J. Hall, removed from the steamer. Three of the trunks were delivered to the doctor. Hyams took the five rope-tied trunks to his own hotel room; he was informed they contained clothing infected with yellow fever and smallpox. He assured the court that he had refused to accept a small valise of elegant shirts which Blackburn wanted him to present to President Lincoln.

In his hotel room Hyams removed the obviously soiled items from the trunks and repacked them. To protect himself from the fever germs, Hyams claimed, he followed Blackburn's advice to chew camphor and smoke strong cigars. Once the trunks were repacked, Hyams and Hall bribed a ship's officer to smuggle them into the United States. The baggage was placed aboard the steamer *Halifax*, behind a sliding panel in the porter's quarters, and seven days later Hyams and the trunks arrived in Boston. After obtaining a room at the Astor House, Hyams said he had the trunks expressed to Philadelphia, New York, Washington, and Norfolk. The trunk marked no. 2 was shipped to the nation's capital, as Blackburn instructed, for the doctor believed there was enough poison in it to "kill at sixty yards."[14] Hyams hauled it to Wall and Company Auction House on Ninth Street and Pennsylvania Avenue and received $100 for the goods. Two trunks had been sent to Norfolk, but when Hyams found he could not take one of them on to New Bern, North Carolina, then under Federal occupation, he made arrangements with a sutler named Myers to dispose of the goods for him. When he read several weeks later of the outbreak of yellow fever at New Bern, he assumed that the sutler had carried out his instructions.

Upon the completion of his mission, Hyams declared, he returned to Toronto and met with Blackburn a few days before the doctor made his second visit to Bermuda. Blackburn refused to pay Hyams until he could produce bills-of-sale from all the auction houses that purchased the clothing. To help Hyams's immediate financial needs, including paying the rent and getting his wife's dresses out of pawn, Blackburn gave Hyams fifty dollars and promised to make arrangements with Jacob Thompson, treasurer for the Confederate agents in Canada, to pay Hyams what was owed to him. Hyams said he later received from Thompson a check for fifty dollars drawn on the Ontario Bank, but all other requests to Dr. Blackburn for payment were either ignored or met with promises for eventual payment larger than the original $60,000. Hyams declared that the doctor even promised to take him to France to meet the emperor, who, because of his interest in Mexico, "would give a million to operate in this way on the American army" if the United States attacked the French-sponsored emperor of Mexico, Maximilian.[15]

The Toronto court also subpoenaed the Reverend Stuart Robinson, who admitted that he had introduced Hyams and Blackburn but told the court that when he later learned that Hyams was not trustworthy, he warned others to avoid him. He had no knowledge, Robinson said, of any of Blackburn's activities. Affidavits from William W. Cleary and W. J.

Hall also were presented. Cleary, Thompson's assistant, admitted knowing Blackburn and said the doctor had told him that although Hyams was a "great rascal," he had employed him to "distribute among the army of the United States clothing which he had prepared . . . at Bermuda, infected with yellow fever."[16] The doctor, said Cleary, had cause to doubt that Hyams had carried out the undertaking and proposed to make another attempt with a more reliable agent. Hall's statement told of helping Hyams transfer some baggage from a mail ship and of making arrangements to have it smuggled into Boston aboard the *Silver Spray*. Difficulties at the Boston customhouse were circumvented, explained Hall, because Hyams bribed an official with a twenty-dollar gold piece. Hall claimed to have no knowledge of the trunks' contents or their final destination. Blackburn, who was ill, did not take the stand.

The circumstantial evidence was damning and even the pro-Rebel press in Canada viewed the scheme as "an outrage against humanity." The *Montreal Gazette* suggested that Blackburn's "overzeal for the cause of his country . . . led him to commit himself to so foul a crime." Northern newspapers that had carried glowing reports of General Sherman's devastating sweep across Georgia called the fever plot "one of the most fiendish plots ever concocted by the wickedness of man" and labeled Blackburn a "hideous devil" who was responsible for the mass murder of women and children at New Bern.[17]

Following the hearing the magistrates bound the doctor over for trial, and bail was set at $8,000. Details of the trial before the assizes court in October 1865 are unavailable, but the *New York Times* reported that Blackburn was acquitted. The original charge of conspiracy to commit murder was changed to violation of Canada's neutrality, for the doctor's attorney reminded the court that according to British law the charge of conspiracy to commit murder could only be levied if the intended victim were a head of state; since insufficient evidence had been introduced to indicate that this was Blackburn's intention, the conspiracy charge was dropped. The violation of neutrality accusation was not proved, for the court was unsure that the trunks of infected clothing had been on Canadian soil; had they been, the Toronto court admitted, it had no jurisdiction over cases involving Nova Scotia.

In an attempt to link Confederate officials at Richmond and the agents in Canada to the plot to murder President Lincoln, Godfrey Hyams was questioned during the assassination plot hearing in late May of 1865. His story was essentially the same as the one told in Toronto, although a few minor details differed and a few embellishments were added. Witnesses were not called to substantiate Hyams's sales in New York, Philadelphia, or Norfolk, but the proprietor of the Washington auction house who purchased trunk number 2 testified that his records contained a listing of the trunk's inventory and a receipt for the money that was paid to Hyams. John Cameron of Montreal told the court that he had been approached by Blackburn in January 1865 to take clothing to northern cities the following spring. His fear of contracting the disease, said Cameron, was greater than his desire to aid the Confederacy or to earn the money that Blackburn promised.

During the assassination trial, testimony given at a secret session seemed to prove that the yellow fever scheme had been sanctioned by officials in Richmond and that the doctor, the Canadian agents, and President Davis plotted with John Wilkes Booth and others to murder Lincoln. Mention was even made of seeing Blackburn in Booth's company on at least one occasion in Montreal, but this and other information concerning Blackburn and the Confederate agents was discounted when the judges learned that a member of the Justice Department had paid a notorious perjurer to present erroneous evidence that would send Davis and the others to the gallows. Interest in prosecuting the absent Blackburn suddenly vanished when it became apparent that Davis could not be linked to the yellow fever "murders." Nevertheless, the murder charge against Blackburn was not withdrawn.

The Blackburns remained in Canada after other agents returned home. The war had cost the doctor his fortune and reputation, and he feared imprisonment if he returned to the states. In the spring of 1866 one of his prewar patients requested a friend in New York to intercede on Blackburn's behalf and present a petition for the doctor's pardon. Concerning the charges that had been levied against his "dear old friend exiled to Canada," the Natchez resident explained that "I honestly do not believe that Doctor Blackburn did any more harm during the late rebellion than a little talking that might have been left unsaid. . . . His trying to run the blockade with a few bales of cotton for the support of his family gave rise to the evil reports against him. . . . It is too cruel and unjust to punish a man when he is not guilty."[18] The request was denied.

In September of 1867 Blackburn addressed a letter to President Andrew Johnson that must have required considerable bravado.

From the dispatch today I see that the fever is prevailing in New Orleans, Galveston and other points to a most fatal extent. General Sheridan telegraphed that the last army surgeon had died at New Orleans. I addressed a letter today to the American Consell [sic] here offering my services to your government without compensation, *and stating my willingness to go at once to any point and render my professional services to the officers and soldiers of the United States, where their surgeons are sick and unable to attend. This letter Consul E. Thurston has enclosed to Gen. Grant, Acting Secretary of War. I have had much experience in the treatment of this disease and feel confident I could render essential service to my suffering and dying countrymen—if it is, Mr. President, consistent with your duty to accept my offer, my conduct shall be such as to meet and merit your approbation.*[19]

Johnson also received a letter from the United States consul in Toronto stating that Blackburn had taken an oath of allegiance to the United States.

In answer to the consul's letter, Secretary of State William H. Seward wrote that he did not believe that the yellow fever "fiend" qualified for a pardon under the most recent amnesty proclamation. "It is not easy to understand how an offence of this character . . . can be supposed even by the felon himself, to be entitled to be regarded as an act of insurrection, rebellion or civil war. The President's proclamation offers no immunity in this case."[20] But Blackburn had not remained in Canada to await an answer to his letter. On September 25 he arrived in Louisville, en route to New Orleans to aid in the care of that city's fever victims. When the fever abated, he and Julia moved to her small plantation in Arkansas, and for six years the physician farmed and practiced medicine near Helena. No evidence has been found to indicate that the charge against Blackburn was ever dropped, but apparently it never was pressed.

The modern sleuth who attempts to determine how much of the yellow fever plot was truth and how much was fabrication is hampered by lack of real evidence. In 1865 the most damaging proof that Blackburn tried to spread yellow fever was the outbreak at New Bern. This evidence can now be discounted, for we know that the disease cannot be spread through contact with contaminated clothing. The credibility of Godfrey Hyams, an inglorious turncoat whose loyalties responded to money rather than to a cause, can be questioned but not ignored, but the statements of the witnesses who appeared before the Bermuda court, the affidavit of William Cleary, and the testimony of the auction house proprietor are hard to disregard. Records kept by the rebel agents in Canada who knew Blackburn were destroyed, and neither the memoirs of the major Confederate leaders nor the autobiographies of his friends and associates in Canada mention the accusations levied against him.

Blackburn's humanitarian efforts before and after the war are incongruent with the charge of deliberate mass murder, but war does bring out the worst in human nature; perhaps the doctor believed that he had the same right to use his skills and knowledge to slay the enemy as had any general. Blackburn's postwar deeds can be construed either as those of a man wishing to atone for past sins or as those of one who had nothing to hide. His only public statement about the charge, made many years later, was that the whole accusation was "too preposterous for intelligent gentlemen to believe."[21]

In the light of modern knowledge about yellow fever, an attempt to spread the pestilence with infected clothing was preposterous. But Blackburn and his contemporaries were ignorant about the cause of Yellow Jack. Had the doctor been arrested and tried by the American authorities, he undoubtedly would have been executed for murdering two thousand persons at New Bern during the 1864 outbreak. He probably was guilty of trying to use his knowledge to aid the Confederacy's desperate struggle against a superior force, but Blackburn certainly was innocent of murder. Only a mosquito can be held responsible for spreading the deadly yellow fever virus.

3

HERO OF HICKMAN

THE BLACKBURNS returned to their native state in the early months of 1873 and made their home at Louisville's finest hotel, the Galt House. The doctor opened an office on West Jefferson and apparently enjoyed a busy and lucrative practice. Because of their family connections and their outgoing personalities, both Julia and Luke became part of the elite social circles of the town. They helped entertain visiting dignitaries, belonged to leading literary circles, and counted among their friends the state's most influential people.

Louisville in 1873 was a prosperous commercial and manufacturing center, and her 100,000 residents enjoyed many modern conveniences not available in most of the commonwealth's urban areas. Seventy miles of gas lines supplied the streets, homes, and businesses with lights; the city waterworks piped water from the Ohio River to homes along the principal streets and avenues; and two city railroad companies provided transportation from the business district to the suburbs. A board of health and a street department were responsible for keeping the city clean, but many parts of the town abounded with "miasmatic conditions." The local papers frequently shamed the health board for permitting animal carcasses to lie in the streets and for allowing an intolerable stench or foul breeze to characterize various districts. In the spring of 1873, when Asiatic cholera slipped through the ineffective quarantine station at New Orleans, the *Courier-Journal* warned residents of the city to clean up those streets that held "as many bad smells now as the people can endure" lest the disease strike Louisville.[1]

Cholera did visit Kentucky in 1873, but most of its victims were residents of small towns who got their drinking water from polluted wells. During the epidemic, which raged throughout the state for three months, the *Courier-Journal* carried articles by prominent local physicians on the cause and prevention of the disease. Most of them were reiterations of the same theories espoused during the state's three previous cholera epidemics. One, by Luke Blackburn, was different. Blackburn warned his readers that impure water caused cholera. During the epidemics of 1833 in Lexington and of 1848-1854 in Mississippi, people who obtained water from concrete-lined cisterns had remained healthy, Blackburn insisted. Where cistern or "pure" river water was unavailable, Blackburn suggested that water be boiled to destroy impurities. His advice was scoffed at by several Louisville physicians, including Theodore S. Bell, a University of Louisville medical professor, who insisted that cholera was a miasmatic disease; boiling water could have no effect on airborne, cholera-producing poisons. Unfortunately, most Kentuckians followed the advice of the better-known Bell, and thousands died from the dreaded disease.

Cholera also visited Memphis during the summer of 1873, and a few weeks after that disease abated, yellow fever was reported in Happy Hollow, a twenty-block area of the city inhabited, according to the *Courier-Journal*, by "negroes, low Irish, goats and hogs."[2] As the pestilence began to spread across the city, attempts were made to counteract the fever-producing pathogens. One hundred barrels of tar were burned in the roadways, and gas was permitted to escape from every street lamp! But some Memphis merchants and the local chapter of the Howard Association, a benevolent society founded in 1837 to aid the South during fever epidemics, doubted the effectiveness of tar and gas and issued pleas for help. The Howards of Mobile were requested to send fifteen nurses, and the businessmen telegraphed Blackburn that his services were needed.

The physician arrived in Memphis on September 23. When the mayor refused to accept his offer to help the sick, Blackburn reported to the Howard office on West Court Street and received a genuine welcome. He learned that most of the cases were confined to Happy Hollow, an area of small retail shops, groceries, saloons, and poorly constructed and overcrowded dwellings. Boardinghouses were filled with sick persons "bound by no ties of kindred or affection," and in the hovellike homes "the sick, the well, the dying and the dead huddled together" with no one to care for them. An earlier attempt by the Howards to establish a yellow fever hospital was squelched by the "ignorant and turbulent classes" of the area, who feared that such a facility would propagate and perpetuate the pestilence in Happy Hollow.[3] Nevertheless, Blackburn and W. T. Watham, a volunteer from Mobile, secured a vacant boardinghouse on a river bluff and set up an infirmary. Opposition to their hospital quickly vanished, for the mayor placed at their disposal a detachment of armed policemen.

Area residents, at first reluctant to use the infirmary, soon filled it to capacity. During the six weeks the disease raged throughout Memphis, 167 patients were treated at the temporary hospital. A large portion of them arrived at the facility in a "moribund condition" and thus the death rate was high—47 percent. Watham attributed the survival of the other patients to Blackburn's "incomparable skill and efficiency" and praised the Kentuckian's "professional knowledge and experience that were combined with sound practical judgment, a diagnostic insight . . . extraordinary capability of physical endurance and a cheerfulness and kindliness of heart."[4]

More than two thousand persons died in Memphis during the 1873 epidemic, but two stories of Blackburn's activities in the besieged city show a less grim side of the ordeal. The memoirs of the Reverend D. A. Quinn, a Catholic priest whose Irish communicants in Happy Hollow were among

Blackburn's patients, praised the doctor's "philanthropy, which was not always confined to marble halls and telephone calls" and told of his sympathies for ten-year-old Mary Sullivan, the sole survivor of a large family. Concerned about the orphan's future, Blackburn purchased a new dress for the child and offered to take her to Louisville.

Gossip quickly spread that Mary was "to be brought up as a lady, sent to a first-class boarding school, and decently portioned for life." When the priest heard what the Protestant doctor proposed, he forbade Mary to go with him. Blackburn visited Quinn, satisfied the priest that his intentions were respectable, and gained permission to take the waif from Memphis providing he sent her to a Catholic seminary. Blackburn agreed. The priest related that Mary went to Louisville with Blackburn, where she was "carried around to all his medical and merchant friends . . . and kept before the public eye for several days" as a publicity gimmick. Blackburn then took Mary to the Sisters of Charity at Nazareth Academy. Quinn and Mary met on a Nashville street eight years later. When he inquired about her benefactor, Mary informed the priest that during her five-year stay at Nazareth the "old thing never paid the poor Sisters a cent for me." Concluded the priest: "As a Protestant I suppose he thought it enough to give her in charge of the Sisters. In truth, I would never consent to let him take the child if I did not believe she was to be educated and portioned for life."[5] Quinn did not speculate what the girl's future might have been had she remained in Happy Hollow.

Both Quinn and the Louisville press reported Blackburn's caning of another doctor on the streets of Memphis. J. M. Ryan, a volunteer from Chicago who professed to be a physician experienced in the treatment of yellow fever, visited one of Blackburn's patients and administered medications of which Blackburn disapproved. When the two men met on the street several hours later, Blackburn accused Ryan of being "nothing more than an old preacher" and "a quack."[6] Tempers flared, additional words were exchanged, and Blackburn caned the man severely with his walking stick.

The bruised Ryan ran for a policeman. Blackburn went immediately to the station house, related his story, and surrendered himself to the authorities, who refused to interfere and told the doctor to "go tend to his patients." The proprietor of the Peabody Hotel, where both men boarded, made inquiries of the authorities and medical society in Chicago and found that Ryan was a defrocked priest. Local physicians, who earlier had chastised Blackburn for his violent deed, thanked the Kentuckian for defending medical integrity against the "Chicago Quack."[7]

The epidemic began to subside in late October and by the end of the first week in November most of Blackburn's patients were convalescing. Before his return to Louisville in mid-November, the people of Memphis presented Blackburn with a silver tray, and a group of Memphis physicians, who accompanied him to the dock to meet his boat, gave him an ebony cane, richly mounted in gold, in token of their appreciation for aid given their stricken brethren.

Blackburn also answered a call from fever victims in the early fall of 1877 when yellow fever struck the community of Fernandina in northeastern Florida. For his services at Fernandina—and at all other towns he aided during his medical career—Blackburn refused to accept compensation or expense money.

After the Florida epidemic several southern newspapers carried lengthy articles in which they told of Blackburn's many acts of charity to communities stricken by the scourge. The *New Orleans Picayune* commented on his prewar career and reminded its readers that Blackburn, not "Beast Butler," had established the first effective quarantine in the Mississippi Valley. Besides aiding American communities, the *Picayune* exaggerated, Blackburn fought the fever in the "Bahamas" during the "late war," for which the British government offered the philanthropist "a silver service and a knighthood." The *Memphis Appeal* declared that the "spirit shown by men going into battle with a sword and gun is cowardice" compared to Blackburn's unflinching aid to fever-ridden communities. "Such a man ought to be canonized as a benefactor of his race. He is *the* Howard of America." The Louisville press compared Blackburn's deeds to those of the biblical Good Samaritan, and a few months later the Kentucky legislature published a resolution saluting the humanitarian's "heroism of kindness and self abnegation."[8] After such flattering notices, it is no wonder that the doctor decided to run for public office.

On February 11, 1878, the *Courier-Journal* announced Blackburn's candidacy for the 1879 Democratic nomination for governor of Kentucky. When and why the doctor decided to solicit the office is unknown. Several of his brothers and brothers-in-law enjoyed successful political careers— Joseph Clay Stiles Blackburn was a strong contender for Speaker of the United States House of Representatives; James Blackburn was a member of the Kentucky Senate; Samuel Churchill had served as Kentucky's secretary of state under governors Helm, Stevenson, and Leslie; and Thomas Churchill was Arkansas's treasurer. Perhaps their enthusiasm for politics was infectious. It is also possible that Jefferson Davis planted the idea when he informed Blackburn and other friends in Kentucky that his own opposition to amnesty should not prevent them from "enjoying whatever benefits may be accorded" from participating in the governmental process.[9]

Blackburn considered the announcement of his candidacy the "most important event of my life," and told his former commander-in-chief that as a candidate he would have the opportunity to "appeal to the people of my native state to expunge from my name that obliquy [*sic*] which the venal press and people of the North put on it at a time when no friend could defend me unless at the peril of his life and liberty." The *Courier-Journal* predicted that Blackburn would "prove no small obstacle in the way of a successful man," but the physician's friends viewed his premature announcement and his ambition as an "indiscreet and hopeless venture," for he would have to compete with astute and well-known politicians.[10]

Nineteenth-century Kentucky provided almost constant

opportunities for political campaigning, for there were few months during which contests for national, state, county, or municipal offices were not in progress. Candidates for gubernatorial positions campaigned for months, speaking sometimes twice a day, as they tried to visit every hill and hollow across the commonwealth. The state's major towns were linked by railroad and steamboat services, but carriage trips over deeply rutted roads to areas in the hinterland were slow and hazardous; some constituents could be reached only after journeying for miles by horse and mule. The expenses involved for travel, meals, and overnight accommodations could be greater than the niggardly salaries paid to state officials.

A political rally was an excuse for merriment among the voters. Major candidates were frequently feted with picnics and barbecues, where good food and strong drink were served in abundance. Following the gastronomical treat, voters listened to an hour or more of fiery oratory filled with accusations and counteraccusations about the opponents and opposing party—of horrors that occurred during the war, of injustices and bayonet rule during Reconstruction, and of corruption and incompetence that characterized men in high places. Nearly every crowd contained a few troublemakers, and fights and free-for-alls were not uncommon among short-tempered, quarrelsome listeners. Even law-abiding citizens, driven to temporary insanity by spirited oratory and liquor, sometimes joined the pugilists. Campaigning was a tiring, expensive, and even dangerous endeavor, especially for a sixty-three-year-old who had no oratorical experience and was a political novice.

Blackburn opened his campaign with a speech at the Owen County Courthouse on March 29 and throughout the spring and summer concentrated his efforts in central Kentucky. A Shelbyville audience heard his views on freedom of the press and his warning that if it was struck down, "you bury in a common grave the liberties of the people and the perpetuity of the government."[11]

To a Frankfort crowd he explained that public office was

not the exclusive preserve of the legal profession; all professions had a contribution to make to good government, he reasoned. Elaborating on this theme before a Fayette County gathering, where many of his listeners supported the yet unannounced Judge William Lindsay, Blackburn suggested that the office should seek the man, but that a man "should not assume the modesty of a blushing school girl."[12] Most of Blackburn's speeches were well attended and the press praised his subject matter, called his arguments "sensible," and compared his delivery to that of his brother Joseph, a born orator whose unfaltering and resounding voice was familiar to Kentuckians. Instead of attempting to clear his name as he had indicated to Davis, the doctor spoke of the nation's monetary difficulties, mentioned the need for prison reforms in Kentucky, and suggested that matters concerning public health demanded attention. He also criticized the Republican party for its scandals, frauds, and harsh treatment of the postwar South.

If elected, Blackburn promised, he would devote his efforts to matters concerning education and public health and would do all possible to "erase local prejudices" across the state. As other candidates were announced, he invited them to participate with him in public debate. Moreover, he vowed that his election to the executive office would "fill to overflowing" his political ambitions, and he asked his opponents to join him in a pledge that they would not use the governorship as a stepping-stone for other political offices.[13]

About the same time Blackburn announced his candidacy, he made a personal appeal before the state legislature and urged it to accept the proposal then being debated to establish a state board of health and to institute emergency provisions for the erection of quarantine stations at the state's border towns and transportation centers. He pleaded with the legislators to instruct Kentucky's delegates to Congress to work for similar measures at the national level. Although his other suggestions received only token attention, the State Board of Health was created in March 1878. The six-member board, appointed by the governor, "advised officers of the government" concerning matters of public health. The board's secretary, its only paid member, served as superintendent of vital statistics; the lawmakers appropriated $2,500 to cover his salary and all annual expenses incurred by the board.[14] Because it had only advisory powers, the infant organization was unable to act effectively when yellow fever began its deadly march up the Mississippi River during the summer of 1878.

The 1878 epidemic was the worst of the postwar period. The disease appeared in the gulf area earlier in the season than usual and reached epidemic proportions along the lower Mississippi by midsummer. Before the disease abated in late October, most of the towns along the Mississippi and Ohio rivers were stricken. An estimated 50,000 fever victims died.

As the South's refugees fled northward, Cairo, Paducah, Columbus, Saint Louis, and Cincinnati closed their doors to them. Blackburn advised Louisville to do likewise. Most Louisvillians, however, believed a quarantine was needless and cruel. Yellow fever had not been diagnosed in Louisville since 1822; the city was immune to the scourge, some argued. Others, who insisted that the malady could not strike so far north, doubted that the 1822 epidemic was yellow fever. Professor Theodore S. Bell, author of many medical monographs, was the major antiquarantine spokesman. Although he had never treated a case of the disease, Bell insisted that it "springs from a local surface," but that the Falls City, "once given to such fevers," had drained her miasma-producing ponds and "never produces a case now."[15] Another medical professor, Lunsford P. Yandell, Jr., admitted to attending only one yellow fever patient in his twenty-year medical career but agreed with Bell that the disease could not appear in Louisville. The city's residents, said Yandell, were in much greater danger from the "lions and tigers and boa constrictors and anacondas which come here in the menageries than they are from the yellow fever refugees from the South. The bars of the cages of these wild beasts are not so safe a protection to us as are the laws of nature governing disease."[16] Since most of the city's physicians agreed with the medical professors, they advised the local board of health to keep the city open to the refugees. Amused by the entire controversy, the *Courier-Journal* carried a ditty that summed up the state's anti-isolationist views.

> *Some cities now this measure take,*
> *From every ill to screen.*
> *A first class case of stomach-ache,*
> *Is put in quarantine.*
> *The day will come, when by this rule,*
> *The present serves to show,*
> *No boy will be allowed in school,*
> *Who dares to stub his toe.*[17]

Kentuckians expressed compassion for stricken neighbors by providing aid for victims of the disease as well as for the refugees who fled from it. Fraternal, social, and religious organizations formed relief societies and offered their services and financial resources to towns devastated by the fever. "Nickel boxes" placed in stores and business establishments collected funds for needed commodities, and Kentucky ingenuity raised money through raffles, lectures, benefit concerts, fairs, festivals, minstrel shows, moonlight railway excursions, and even mule races. In a three-week period about $40,000 was collected. Kentucky's fever victims would receive a large portion of this money.

As the disease crept closer to the commonwealth, Louisville's newspapers detailed distressing news of the epidemic's progress from New Orleans, to Baton Rouge, to Natchez, to Vicksburg, and to Memphis. Blackburn predicted that the epidemic would continue to spread northward until frost. Although his friends urged him "not to abandon his canvass at a time when every effort was necessary for success," the doctor canceled all speaking engagements in mid-August and announced that he was ready to go "whenever and wherever called to the aid of my fellow beings or fellow citizens . . . regardless of the dangers incurred or the labors required." Bell continued to assure Louisvillians that they were safe, for their city was "one of the cleanest on earth."[18] Despite the professor's guarantee, some residents of the Falls City "disinfected" their property, and the mayor instructed the local police to report any miasmatic conditions to the street department.

Many of the South's refugees were ill when they arrived in Louisville, and the city made provisions for them. A specially devised signal system informed the town's doctors when sick passengers disembarked at the depots and wharves; the ill were quickly transferred to City Hospital or to the temporary fever facility erected on the grounds of Saint John's Eruptive Hospital. Two nuns and several medical students provided most of the nursing care for fever sufferers and local physicians prescribed their favorite remedies, but only Blackburn had any practical knowledge of the disease. His suggested treatment was simple and was carried in the newspapers with those of other physicians: bed rest, the use of blankets to promote sweating, crushed ice to allay thirst, tea, ale, and brandy to stimulate the circulation, and chicken broth and cornmeal gruel to provide nourishment.

Louisville's first fever cases were reported among refugees, but the disease also afflicted residents, most of whom lived within a block of a water-filled sinkhole near the railroad depot. The newspaper tried to prevent panic by reiterating Bell's statement that the ill were suffering from malignant remittent fever, but in late September the press finally admitted that Blackburn was correct—indigenous yellow fever did exist in Louisville. Fortunately, the disease never became epidemic. The physician in charge of the temporary hospital recorded fifty local cases and twenty-eight deaths. Nevertheless, a Cincinnati newspaper reported that disease ravaged the Falls City and that her panic-stricken residents were fleeing. Saint Louis and several other towns immediately placed quarantines against all goods arriving from Louisville. The *Courier-Journal* explained Cincinnati's "malicious lie" as an attempt to harm her rival's commercial activities; the Queen City, said the Louisville paper, should be renamed the Quarantine City for refusing succor to those in need.

Bowling Green also suffered indigenous fever cases. An important transportation center located at the junction of the Memphis branch with the main line of the Louisville and Nashville Railroad, the town welcomed her southern neighbors. Illnesses similar to yellow fever appeared among residents living near the railroad station, but town officials denied the presence of the disease. When someone sent an appeal to Blackburn for his help, the local board of health immediately refuted the plea. Twenty-six of Bowling Green's five thousand residents died of yellow fever during a six-week period, a tragic number but small compared to the figure recorded in western Kentucky.

Early in August the *Courier-Journal* reported that two children who regularly sold apples to steamboat passengers at the Mississippi River port of Hickman had died of yellow fever. Two weeks later another article told of additional cases but quoted Hickman's physicians who denied that the disease was Yellow Jack. Throughout the month of August rumors and denials appeared in the Louisville paper, but on September 5 Hickman's mayor telegraphed the president of the State Board of Health that yellow fever was epidemic and requested Dr. Blackburn's immediate help. Blackburn also received a wire from the mayor, and he volunteered to go to western Kentucky as the board's official representative and direct the necessary medical and nursing care. The doctor arrived at the river town two days later to find more than fifty persons, including three of the area's six physicians, mortally ill. Most of the town's 1,500 residents had fled, some of them to the nearby farm of Dr. J. M. Alexander, who set up army tents to accommodate persons running from the pestilence. A state of near hysteria prevailed among the remaining 350 residents, the majority of whom were poor, white inhabitants of a low area along the river known as "Old Hickman."

Blackburn organized relief committees to dispense food,

clothing, and bedding; he converted the Commercial Hotel into a hospital and instructed a group of women in nursing techniques. Cleanup crews disinfected the town with lime and burning tar. The community's black residents, few of whom had been affected by the disease, volunteered their services to Blackburn to shroud and bury the dead, and hastily organized but efficient squads of Negroes guarded vacated homes and businesses against vandalism. Blackburn reported to the board of health that additional volunteers were needed and sent to the mayor of Louisville a request for mattresses, blankets, and foodstuffs. Before the disease abated, sympathetic Kentuckians donated more than $12,000 worth of supplies to Hickman.

In answer to Blackburn's plea for additional personnel, three physicians, several nurses, a telegraph operator, and a druggist hastened to the river town. Despite his warning that volunteers should be acclimated, and thus perhaps immune to the scourge, all were from areas previously untouched by the disease, and most of them contracted yellow fever and died. Among the volunteers who arrived in mid-September were Drs. Daniel Gober of Louisville, John Loy Cook of Henderson, and J. D. Leslie of Lincoln, Nebraska. Cook was "anxious to demonstrate his theories of the disease," and despite Blackburn's warnings that he and the others not overexpose themselves, especially at night, to the "death-dealing contagion or infection of yellow fever sick rooms," they gave round-the-clock care to their patients "without fear of consequences or hope of reward."[19]

By late September it appeared that the disease was abating at Hickman. Leaving the town in the care of the volunteer physicians and well-trained nursing teams, Blackburn traveled to Chattanooga to pay a professional call on poet-priest Abram Joseph Ryan, and then went to Martin, Tennessee, to organize nursing teams for Memphis, where the disease was unusually malignant. Ten days after his departure from western Kentucky, the doctor received word that yellow fever had broken out with renewed force at Hickman, had been diagnosed at Fulton, and had stricken the doctors of both towns. Blackburn returned immediately to Hickman to discover Cook dead and Leslie, Gober, and most of the nurses severely ill. For several weeks he worked day and night as the only physician within the area. Despite a hectic schedule in which he frequently visited thirty patients per day Blackburn never admitted fatigue. He promised that as long as fresh horses were available he would attend to everyone who needed his help. He not only treated the sick, but he also built fires, fixed coffee, prepared food, and "bathed the feet" of his patients—black or white. The *Paducah Sun* praised his unusual compassion for black patients as "one of the grandest acts of a life that is replete with grand acts." Blackburn became the hero of the Purchase area. On October 18 the masthead of the *Paducah Daily News* carried Blackburn's name as its favorite candidate for governor; a week later the *Union City Chronicle* declared that Kentucky could not give the doctor "a more fitting reward" than her governorship.[20]

The first frost appeared in southern Kentucky on October 17 and shortly thereafter Blackburn announced the disease's abatement in Hickman. The ill were convalescing and no new cases had been reported. The epidemic was over, but it had taken the lives of more than 162 residents of the Hickman-Fulton area, was fatal to all but one of the local physicians and two volunteers who went to the river town, and had crippled trade and commerce in the area. Only for Luke Blackburn did the cloud of death contain a silver lining.

Blackburn visited several towns in Mississippi before he returned to Louisville. His arrival in the Falls City in late October was marked by a gala reception at the Galt House. In response to the flowery remarks in his honor, Blackburn assured his admirers that he had only performed his duties as a Kentuckian and insisted that the real heroes of the epidemic were the physicians and nurses who gave their lives while fighting the pestilence.

For several weeks after his return, Blackburn enjoyed treatment generally reserved for a victorious military hero.

He was the subject of poems and resolutions and received an impressive array of costly gifts. A group of Louisville ladies gave him a solid silver and porcelain model ship laden with flowers; Louisville's refugees from Memphis presented an elegant diamond-studded medal; the grateful father of a fever victim from Memphis expressed his emotions with a small gold watch fob; and a gold-headed cane was given by admiring students at the Louisville Medical College, where he served as a member of the board of trustees. The most lavish display of love and appreciation came from the Kentucky communities Blackburn had served. On November 7 citizens of Hickman, Fulton, and Paducah gathered at the latter town to honor their hero. Street banners, a brass band, a glittering reception, a formal dance, and the presentation of a superbly crafted, engraved gold medal feted the man whose "heroic devotion to the people of Hickman, Kentucky and other southern cities during the plague of 1878" had won the respect and admiration of the state. A Bluegrass newspaper wryly reported that the doctor now possessed "almost as many badges and medals as a French field marshall."[21]

Blackburn's receptions at campaign gatherings throughout the remainder of the gubernatorial campaign were similar to his welcome at Paducah; bands, banners, and cheering crowds greeted the Hero of Hickman. The general format of the physician's speeches was unchanged by the epidemic. No mention was made by him of his medical activities. His remarks resembled those of any politician—critical comments about the opposition party and vague promises about his own intentions. The man who "looked like a governor"uttered few personal invectives against his opponents for the Democratic nomination—Lieutenant Governor John Cox Underwood of Bowling Green and former Congressman Thomas Lauren Jones of Campbell County.[22] He did, however, pay unusually flattering attention to the ladies, and, although they could not vote, they flocked to hear him.

The appearances of the gubernatorial candidates were

scheduled to predate or coincide with county conventions. At the conventions, usually held on the courthouse lawn, local residents decided which candidate would command the votes of the county's delegates to the party's state convention. The man with the largest number of supporters present at the local meeting received all of the county's votes. Recruiting techniques for these supporters varied, but few illegal or devious means were left untried. Inadequate publication of the county convention, importation of nonresidents and other unqualified voters, the influence of promises, threats, physical force, free liquor—all were employed. Prior to September 1878, Underwood was the favored candidate. Blackburn's activities during the fever epidemic, however, diminished Underwood's chances for the nomination, and thus the lieutenant governor and his political friends apparently felt justified in using whatever means were necessary to regain the advantage and win delegates. Underwood's rallies were notorious for the presence of excessive amounts of liquor. In reference to the vote-getting technique of Underwood and others, a Glasgow newspaper lamented that to "get a man's vote, he must be treated well. About five or six times, just before voting. . . . Mr. John Barleycorn is the most influential cesspool of Kentucky politics."[23]

The county conventions for southcentral Kentucky were held in December and January; both candidates concentrated their efforts during the late fall and early winter in Underwood's home district. Underwood admonished his audiences against hiring a carpenter to do a blacksmith's work, a merchant to prescribe medicine, or a doctor to interpret the law. It was absurd, said the civil engineer, to believe that a doctor was qualified to attend to matters of state. In answer to Underwood's statement Blackburn warned his listeners to beware of ambitious politicians.

In a letter marked confidential, Underwood informed a friend that Blackburn's speech at Bowling Green in mid-November was "full of egotism, bombast, self adulation, self conceit and all such stuff—nauseating in the extreme. . . .

The thing fell flat," and labeled the humanitarian a "blatant old blather-skite with not only no education but no
sense. . . . He is a fraud—He is too sorry even to be a first
class fraud." In contrast to Underwood's evaluation, the
Courier-Journal reported that the doctor's Bowling Green
audience composed "one of the largest and most enthusiastic
crowds in the city's history." It was his third speech of the
day, the paper said, but the sixty-three-year-old doctor
"spoke with the fire of youth and kept his audience perfectly
for one-and-a-half hours."[24]

Despite Blackburn's popularity several of the southcentral counties pledged their delegates to Underwood. The
Louisville Age lamented that the people's wishes were not
always represented by those who cast the nominating votes.
The *Hickman Courier* warned machinators to "proceed
with caution when they go against the will of the people."[25]

The campaign in western Kentucky was an easy victory
for Blackburn. Many Purchase residents had earlier declared that they would vote for the doctor in the state election even if he did not receive the Democratic nomination,
and the local press predicted that not a single area voice
would be raised against Blackburn's nomination. Underwood graciously admitted to a crowd at Princeton that
Blackburn had the advantage in southwestern Kentucky, at
which a Blackburn supporter exclaimed that residents of the
area "breathed the vital air . . . by the grace of Dr. Blackburn."[26] Nevertheless, there was an attempt to influence the
Princeton convention to support Underwood. A correspondent for a Louisville paper reported that Underwood and
his "gang" dragged and pulled men across the courthouse
yard so that they would be counted among the lieutenant
governor's supporters. The Underwoodites "stooped be-
neath the dignity of a gentleman," scorned the reporter.[27]

Irregularities perpetrated by a Blackburn supporter at the
Ballard County convention spurred Underwood to other
questionable activities. To his business partner, Underwood
complained that this convention was called "by the old out-
law [Oscar] Turner" who did not adequately publicize it

and "managed things entirely to suit himself—all in Blackburn's interests." In the same letter in which he criticized the Ballard countian, Underwood instructed his correspondent to "do all things possible" to manipulate the Edmonson County convention, for he needed the votes to counteract Blackburn's easy victory in the Jefferson County convention.[28]

As the campaign progressed, Blackburn's popularity became increasingly obvious. On March 25 Underwood withdrew from the race, admitting that public opinion for the physician was "like an avalanche [that] has swept over every part of the state."[29] With this announcement Underwood's political career ended, and Blackburn's nomination was assured.

Blackburn's campaign against Thomas Jones was less lively, for the bulk of Jones's support was in a small area of northern Kentucky. Jones did not begin to campaign in earnest until the early months of 1879; by then it was obvious that Blackburn was the people's favorite and that underhanded tactics would not succeed in counteracting his popularity. Like those of Blackburn, Jones's addresses criticized the national Republican party; his sole personal comment concerning the doctor was to doubt his compliance with Kentucky's six-year residency requirement. The physician assured Jones that he had been a property owner and taxpayer in Kentucky since 1860, which technically qualified him as a "resident." Only one incident accompanied a Blackburn-Jones rally: at Independence an overenthusiastic mob and a verbal battle between two candidates for superintendent of public instruction provoked near pandemonium at the Kenton County convention—apparently not an unusual occurrence for that county.

Perhaps the most important factors in Blackburn's successful campaign were the absence of a dynamic, widely known opponent and the belief of the state's professional politicians that the newcomer to the political arena would be more easily manipulated than Underwood or Jones. Henry Watterson, editor of Kentucky's most influential newspaper, was the doctor's friend; support by the *Courier-Journal* with its flattering coverage of the humanitarian's activities during the epidemic and the campaign assured Blackburn's bid. Reports in the Louisville paper were reiterated by local newssheets, thus spreading his fame. Only a few of the state's papers questioned Blackburn's motives for halting his canvass and going to Hickman or openly wondered why the physician did not aid the Deep South during the early epidemic when her fever-ridden towns were crying for medical help. And few papers questioned the advisability of rewarding Blackburn's humanitarian efforts with the governorship. The *Carlisle Mercury* suggested that perhaps Blackburn's activities at Hickman were prompted by ambition rather than philanthropy. A northern Kentucky paper also pondered the doctor's motives when it observed that politicians received what they justly deserved "in this wicked world," but philanthropists were supposed to be rewarded in the hereafter. Why, asked the *Newport Local*, was the doctor more interested in "going to Frankfort than to Heaven?"[30]

The Democratic state convention opened May 1 in Louisville. Dominated as usual by former Confederates, the two-day meeting was filled with talk of the "noble cause" and of the injustices Kentucky suffered during the war and Reconstruction. A Republican witness to the affair reported that the constant waving of the "bloody shirt" compelled him to "rinse the taste of rebellion" from his mouth with bourbon.[31] Blackburn's nomination by Basil Duke was accepted by acclamation, and the remainder of the ticket was composed of veteran politicians and former Confederates. A Hopkinsville paper praised the Democrats for selecting a humanitarian rather than a politician for their gubernatorial candidate and predicted that he would capture a large percentage of the Republican black vote; he freed his few slaves at the beginning of the war and had always exhibited a special compassion for members of the black race. The *Louisville Medical News* claimed that Blackburn's nomination "sheds honor . . . upon the profession," for although other doctors had served in political posts, "we know of no other instance where a doctor has been given the highest office in the gift of the people as a reward for professional services." The *Courier-Journal* told its readers that the entire Democratic ticket was so good that "one almost regrets we have not an enemy better worth such a licking as they are going to get," and described the Republican gubernatorial candidate, Walter Evans of Hopkinsville, as a man of "little presence and no dignity—destitute of personal magnetism."[32] Because of the state's postwar, anti-Republican sentiments, Evans's success against any Democrat would have been doubtful. Against the Hero of Hickman, said the April 11 *Courier-Journal*, it was a "fruitless and blind hope" comparable to Ponce de Leon's search for the fountain of youth.

A few weeks after his nomination Blackburn retired to a resort at Crab Orchard Springs, and the party's banner throughout the remainder of the campaign was "defended against the onslaught of the Republicans" by the candidate for attorney general, P. W. "Wat" Hardin, a spellbinding orator.[33] Throughout the summer Hardin and Evans delivered many speeches, most of which dealt with national rather than state issues. Hardin claimed that Evans, who refused to debate with him, was "warped in his judgment and swayed in his convictions by partisan prejudices" because he praised the Republicans for crushing the "heresy of state rights" and for approving of "federal usurpation of rights and powers" never delegated to the national government. The major portion of Hardin's oratory, however, concerned the presidential election of 1876 and the Republicans' "fraudulent" dealings that "cheated" Samuel J. Tilden of his "rightful victory."[34]

Evans, who lauded Republican presidents Grant and Hayes, claimed that the Democratic party had no principles, was responsible for starting the Civil War, and was perpetuating the hatreds that had divided the nation eighteen years earlier. While speaking before a Princeton audience that contained a large group of Negroes, Evans suggested that he would vote for any black man who ran for office—an idea that was regarded as nearly treasonous by the majority of white Kentucky voters, regardless of their party affiliation. Despite the verbiage expended, the campaign was a relatively quiet affair in Kentucky. Democratic newspapers urged all eligible voters to go to the polls, for complacency would weaken the party.

Shortly after his retreat to Crab Orchard, Kentuckians were informed that Blackburn's disappearance from the campaign was precipitated by an "extreme inflammation of the eyes and throat."[35] It is quite possible that the months of vigorous campaigning and his fatiguing activities the previous autumn had impaired the overweight, elderly candidate's health. It is also conceivable that Blackburn preferred not to take up Evans's challenge to a series of debates, for although the physician earlier had urged all candidates to join him in public discussions of the issues, he successfully avoided this confrontation by pleading ill health when Jones accepted his offer. Blackburn's seclusion at the resort may also be explained by the news stories in an Ohio newspaper.

A few days after Blackburn's nomination the Republican *Cincinnati Gazette*, which for years had used the economic and political rivalry between Cincinnati and Louisville as an excuse for scandalmongering, carried an article about a Doctor Blackburn of Civil War fame. The *Gazette's* readers were reminded that a Doctor Blackburn had been brought to trial in Toronto in May of 1865 for violating Canadian neutrality by importing, from Bermuda to the United States via Halifax, trunks of clothing infected with yellow fever. Could this be the same Blackburn who now campaigned for governor of Kentucky? The paper urged Blackburn to answer its inquiry. When no reply appeared, the *Gazette* set out to prove that they were the same, and throughout the remainder of the campaign and during the early months of Blackburn's administration, the Cincinnati paper conducted one of the most determined character assassinations in the history of American journalism.

The paper's "Blackburn Department" published a daily column of rumors, letters, and other "evidence" concerning

Blackburn's war activities. Letters from Bermuda and Canada were quoted, describing the Blackburn who visited there as "fat and good tempered," a "large-bodied blusterer," and a man of above medium size with rather large features, florid complexion and blue eyes.[36] Articles in Bermuda papers relating the trial of Edward Swan were copied, and Godfrey Hyams's testimony was extracted from old Toronto and New York newspapers and records of the assassination trial. The *Gazette* even tried to obtain interviews with three of Blackburn's former associates in Canada—William Cleary, Stuart Robinson, and Godfrey Hyams. Cleary, then a Covington judge, refused to talk to the reporter, and Hyams, a resident of Hopkinsville, offered a few critical comments about Robinson but said nothing about the yellow fever plot. Robinson, pastor of Louisville's Second Presbyterian Church, predicted that Blackburn would be a good governor but declared he knew nothing about the doctor's war activities. The *Gazette*'s exposés were echoed by the northern press. What had been a rather quiet political affair in Kentucky suddenly commanded national attention as Kentucky and her hero were pelted with abuse and ridicule.

Many of the comments carried by northern newspapers bordered on the ludicrous. A Canton, Ohio, paper suggested that if Kentucky elected Dr. Blackburn, she should be forced to secede from the Union. The *Philadelphia Press* besought someone to remove the sacred remains of Henry Clay from Kentucky's polluted soil; and a Chicago daily predicted that Kentuckians would even vote for John Wilkes Booth if the assassin were still alive. Republican newspapers contended that only Democrats would nominate a "fiend" and "mass murderer" for a high political office, but northern Democrats argued that it was typical of southern Democrats to elevate the worst monster since the Emperor Nero to a governor's chair. Relating that the doctor had written to someone of his "soar throat," a Cincinnati reporter described Blackburn as an uneducated charlatan who "murdered his English and misspelled the simplest words" and as an "ignoramus" who managed to gather "enough delegates from the backwoods counties" to secure the nomination but was then forbidden to speak in public lest he harm his party. Another Ohio paper surmised that "Dr. Blackvomit" probably was the best citizen Kentucky had, but feared that the attacks would elevate him in the South's estimation to the same level as that enjoyed by the "traitor" Jefferson Davis.[37]

Throughout the months of sordid name-calling and generally petty behavior, Blackburn remained silent. The *Courier-Journal* answered the *Gazette*'s inquiry by saying that "sworn testimony of Republican pimps, perjurers and murderers" was not worth the notice of "honorable men." The editor of a Lexington paper claimed he was fired by the stockholders for reprinting an article from the Cincinnati paper, but most of the state's newssheets, even those edited by Republicans, ignored the *Gazette*'s meddling. Perhaps Kentucky's Republicans agreed with the *Courier-Journal* that the *Gazette* "persistently lied about Kentucky all the time and under all circumstances" and refused to give credence to the accusation.[38] It may be that the Republicans hoped that Blackburn's silence on the matter would be considered an admission of guilt, or feared that attacks on him by Kentuckians would force him to refute the charges and thereby gain additional support. It is also possible that the idea simply was too farfetched for anyone to believe about the beloved Hero of Hickman. Whatever the reason, the Catlettsburg *Central Methodist* dismissed the diatribes by stating that all politics were "calculated to corrupt the voter."[39] Henry Watterson later confirmed that the story of Blackburn's Civil War activities was known in the state, but said that the majority of those who knew of them either approved of the attempt to take the horrors of war to northern civilians or really did not care what had occurred fifteen years earlier during the bitter and bloody struggle.

Kentuckians ignored the suggestion that Blackburn killed his enemies with yellow fever and remembered only that he spent many years of his life protecting his fellowman from the scourge. On a sultry day in mid-August of 1879, Kentucky voters went to the polls to choose their twenty-eighth governor. As each voter approached the voting officer, he cast his ballot viva voce, loud and clear, and watched the officer record it. Blackburn received 43,000 more votes than Evans, for the largest Democratic majority since 1868. The party's politicos were joyful, for they believed that the governor's mansion would be inhabited by a puppet. The victorious Democrats, including the recovered but forty-pounds-slimmer governor-elect, celebrated the victory a few days later at Crab Orchard Springs. Watterson would later brag that his newspaper had made Blackburn's election possible, and another friend jokingly told the physician that since he was just a "damned old fool," Julia would have to attend to most matters of state.[40] Watterson and the others soon would discover that Blackburn was his own man.

4

GOVERNOR
OF KENTUCKY

Tuesday, September 2, was Blackburn's inaugural day, and, despite an ominous-looking sky, more than 5,000 of his constituents flocked to Frankfort to participate in the festivities. The swearing-in ceremony was to be held on the State House grounds under the hundred-year-old "inaugural elm tree." A large grandstand, erected for the occasion, had been decorated by the women of Frankfort with evergreens, floral arrangements, and banners. Business establishments and homes throughout the town also were adorned with banners and bunting, giving the town a bright, festive appearance. Even Frankfort's two fire engines had been "garnished" for the occasion, but an alarm the night before left their adornments in disrepair and the streets strewn with their "wrecked roses." Other well-laid plans also went awry.

A special train carrying six hundred Louisvillians and the governor-elect's private party to Frankfort arrived nearly an hour late. As Blackburn and party disembarked, a light rain began to fall. Undaunted by the dampness, two hundred brightly uniformed, high-stepping Louisville militiamen and a brass band accompanied the governor-elect to the executive mansion to collect outgoing Governor James Mc-

Creary and escort the celebrities to the Capitol Hotel. A brief welcome was tendered by the city officials, and then the lengthy procession continued to the nearby State House yard, where thousands of well-wishers had already assembled. Just as the entourage arrived at its destination, a cloudburst sent spectators, musicians, militiamen, and dignitaries scurrying for cover; in his haste to find shelter, Blackburn lost his prepared address. After some delay the ceremony was moved to the auditorium in Major Hall. Blackburn's muddy speech was found, but the grandstand's floral arrangements were too bedraggled to salvage and the musicians too scattered to reassemble. Thus, without musical fanfare or aesthetic trimmings, Luke Blackburn took the oath of office before a "steamy" crowd of several thousand persons who were crammed into a room designed to hold fifteen hundred.

The inaugural ceremony was brief. An invocation and a few comments by Governor McCreary preceded Blackburn's remarks. Thanking the people of Kentucky for fulfilling his political ambition, the physician promised to use his executive powers to improve conditions at the nearby state penitentiary and his influence to promote harmony throughout the state. The time had come, Blackburn informed his listeners, for Americans of all sections and political affiliations to "turn with scorn, contempt and loathing from those blatant political tricksters . . . who, for their unholy and selfish ends, continually excite sectional bitterness and hate." Chief Justice W. L. Pryor of the Court of Appeals administered the oath of office, and after a few words from Indiana Governor James D. "Blue Jeans" Williams (so nicknamed because of his usual attire) and a benediction, the new governor retired to the executive office and was invested with the Great Seal of Kentucky.[1]

Festivities continued throughout the afternoon and evening, despite torrential rains. Blackburn held a small, impromptu reception in the late afternoon for some of his close associates. That evening he and seven hundred others, an "assemblage of beauty and elegance such as has seldom been the boast of this city," dined at the Capitol Hotel and attended the magnificent ball in the hotel's ballroom.[2]

Two days later the Democrats of Fayette County held a barbecue in Blackburn's honor at Hostetter's Grove, two miles outside of Lexington. It was a glorious, sunny day, and a thousand persons were there to greet the Blackburns, hear several of the state's best orators praise the new governor, and to enjoy the burgoo, barbecued mutton, and Kentucky bourbon. After the picnic Blackburn traveled to Cincinnati to represent his state at the Industrial Exposition and to meet President Rutherford B. Hayes and his companions and accompany them back to Kentucky. The new governor and his guests visited High Bridge, attended the races in Lexington, and toured some of the points of interest in Lexington and Louisville. Blackburn's administration was off to a propitious beginning.

A few days after the inauguration the Blackburns began the arduous task of making a home out of the old governor's mansion on High Street. Erected in 1797, the drafty, twelve-room brick dwelling had once been one of the most pretentious houses in Frankfort, but by the 1870s it was in a shabby, dilapidated condition and was without modern conveniences. The flooring for the ground story was "propped up with large timbers . . . on account of the lowering [settling] of the walls," and the rotten shingle roof was dangerous. The area adjacent to the home was poorly drained and cluttered with unsightly commercial buildings; the state penitentiary was across the street. Governor McCreary had referred to the house as a "rat-trap," and summer visitors commented on the stench from the nearby prison that permeated the house and grounds. A committee of the 1878 legislature proclaimed the house "unfit for the residence of the Governor of Kentucky."[3]

In April of 1878 Harry I. Todd had offered to the state as a governor's home his nineteen-room residence on the corner of Wapping and Wilkinson streets. Located in the healthiest and most desirable area of the capital, the almost-

Old Governor's Mansion.
Courtesy of Kentucky Historical Society

new $60,000 brick edifice was all that the governor's home should have been. Todd proposed to exchange his modern home for $15,000 in cash and the property on which the old governor's home was located, a veritable bargain for the state. But the 1878 legislature refused to accept the offer, for the land had been donated to the state and there was some question about the legality of selling it. When a proposal to purchase Todd's home for $20,000 was made in the 1880 legislature, bedlam resulted. Lawmakers who were busy introducing bills for "the relief of" every indigent voter they could think of suddenly became penny-pinching economists. Rather than spend money for a new home for the governor, many legislators agreed with an Owensboro paper's suggestion that the existing "old trap" should be sold and that future governors should provide their own quarters. It was not necessary for the executive to have a palatial dwelling, said the Owensboro paper. "Let our governors cease to be dispensers of wine and wassail—mere stewards of the feast—and devote their entire attention to the legitimate duties of their office."[4] A senator from the mountain area even suggested that the state should save the taxpayers' dollars by selling to the highest bidder all of the state-owned buildings, including the State House. Although the solons decided not to evict the governor—or themselves—into the cold, their attitude toward the governor's mansion typified sentiments of the era concerning expenditures of state funds. The thin veneer of elegance that would grace the old governor's house for another thirty years was due to the talents and skills of Kentucky's first ladies rather than any desire of lawmakers to provide a residence in keeping with the prestige of the office and the social responsibilities that went with it.

The Blackburns abandoned the custom of holding Monday-night levees for members of the legislature, but they nevertheless entertained frequently and lavishly, especially during the legislative sessions. Their New Year's Day receptions, which exhibited the "easy grace that bespeaks of the influence of gentle blood," the annual Governor's Ball, a formal wedding reception for Lieutenant Governor and Mrs. James E. Cantrill, and many informal dances were the highlights of the Frankfort social season.[5] Perhaps their most interesting affair was a December 1881 frolic during which a thousand guests dined and danced at the governor's home from 4 P.M. to midnight. At the combination barbecue and hoe-down the ladies completed a lavender silk quilt, the young people pulled taffy, and young and old consumed a sizable quantity of smoked possum, roasted pig, and apple toddy. A group of elderly black fiddlers provided music and called the reels. The evening's most popular dancer was ninety-eight-year-old Dr. Christopher Columbus Graham, Jo Blackburn's father-in-law. The *New York Times* carried a description of the unusual party and informed its readers that although the elderly Graham had not danced in nearly eighty years, "it was wonderful to watch the way he cut the pigeon wing" at the "Kentucky governor's quilting party."[6]

As the commonwealth's official host, representative, and spokesman, Blackburn entertained numerous dignitaries who visited the state—two United States presidents, three governors, a Canadian official, and an Irish patriot—and dedicated monuments, laid cornerstones, opened county fairs, made graduation addresses, and delivered the state's greeting to various societies and organizations that met in Louisville and Lexington. He also represented the state at President Garfield's funeral, attended industrial expositions in Cincinnati, Atlanta, and Nashville, was a special guest at the inauguration of Arkansas's governor Thomas Churchill (Julia's brother), and was feted by Memphis during her 1881 celebration of the city's recent escape from yellow fever. Expenses for all of these travels, as well as those for entertaining, domestic help, and so forth, came from the governor's salary, a modest $5,000, which was reduced to $4,000 by the 1880 legislature.

Although he enjoyed entertaining and traveling, Blackburn's favorite recreational activity was to attend horse races, and he was a familiar figure at Louisville's Churchill

Downs (named for Julia's brothers who donated the land), and at the Lexington track. Blackburn's love for horses and horse racing was appropriately emphasized by an interesting coincidence during his first year in office. The nation's number-one racehorse in 1880 was a Tennessee stallion named Luke Blackburn. Foaled in 1874, the colt was named in honor of the man who aided Memphis during the 1873 epidemic. Blackburn was proud of his namesake and liked to joke about the pitiful hunks of horseflesh that had been named after other state politicians. A horse called Jo Blackburn, the governor pointed out as his blue eyes twinkled, was "tried and found wanting," and a "perfect equine prodigy named Jim Beck" (United States senator from Kentucky) failed to get out of the starter's gate. But, bragged Blackburn, an "underdeveloped, ungainly colt" named Luke Blackburn became monarch of the racetrack. When the stallion visited Louisville in September of 1880, Blackburn presented him with a handsome red and gold blanket upon which was embroidered, "Luke Blackburn King of the Turf."[7]

Despite his travels and social activities Blackburn spent most of his time attending to matters of state. When the weather permitted it, the portly doctor walked to work along the "Governor's Alley" that connected his home to the state buildings three blocks away. The first floor of the new "fire proof" stone building (Old Capitol Annex) adjacent to the State House contained the executive offices. Completed in 1872 the building was to have been the east wing of a new capitol, but the rest of the proposed edifice was never constructed. From nine to three on weekdays Blackburn and Jake Corbett (the governor's nephew and private secretary) were at their desks to greet the public and to attend to state business. The executive received as many as fifty letters daily, which were laboriously answered by the governor or Corbett. Corbett's duties included working as the governor's only clerk and keeping the books for the state's various charitable institutions. Most of Blackburn's time was consumed greeting the public, preparing messages, reviewing legislation passed by the General Assembly (a relatively large portion of which he vetoed), and studying the various petitions and requests addressed to him. Although the office closed at midafternoon, the governor was often at his desk in the evening, answering letters and studying bills that required his signature. One cold wintry evening when he was working past ten o'clock, the janitor assumed that everyone had gone home, locking the doors between the executive suite and the rest of the building. Finding himself a "prisoner in his own castle," the governor yelled out the window at passersby until he attracted the attention of a gentleman who obtained a ladder and helped his chief down from the twelve-foot-high window ledge. The next day Frankfort was buzzing about the old governor's "stealing home at that late hour and impressing his wife with the manifold duties that detained him from the cheerful fireside of the Executive Mansion."[8]

Throughout his governorship Blackburn's closest advisor was his secretary of state. Shortly after the August election he had announced that Samuel Churchill was his choice for the office. When a reporter from the *Louisville Commercial* suggested that the appointment of his brother-in-law was unwise, Blackburn supposedly told him, "By G-d, I intend to make the appointment in spite of h--l." The *Breckinridge News*, perhaps with tongue in cheek, concluded that the governor was following the Bible's admonition that "he that provideth not for his own household is worse than a heathen," but the *Mayfield Democrat* warned that former President U. S. Grant "rendered himself odious by such a course."[9] The *Courier-Journal* reminded Kentuckians that Blackburn's choice for the position was a wise one, for Churchill was eminently qualified. He had previously served, and ably, as secretary of state under governors Stevenson, Leslie, and Helm. He would be a valuable aide, said the Louisville paper, to a governor whose political acumen was limited. When Churchill resigned his office in the spring of 1880 because of ill health, James Blackburn replaced him. The governor's younger brother had served two terms in the state senate and was knowledgeable about state affairs. He, too, was an able advisor, but the appointment upset the state's spoilsmen.

Next door to the new structure that housed the offices of the governor and other state officials was the State House, which was nearly dwarfed by a large American flag that flew over it. Completed in 1830, the magnificent Greek Revival building designed by Gideon Shryock housed the Court of Appeals and both chambers of the legislature. The court rooms were on the ground floor, and the double, self-supporting stone staircase that dominated the main hall of the first floor led up to the legislative chambers. The one hundred representatives to the house met in the large room across the back of the building. Decorated with portraits of Washington, Lafayette, and Daniel Boone, the room was filled with well-rubbed mahogany desks and was lit by a brass and crystal gas chandelier; a coal-burning fireplace warmed it. The senate chamber had been redecorated a few years earlier and was bright and attractive, outfitted similarly to the house. A life-size portrait of William Henry Harrison hung over the speaker's chair, and on the walls to the left were large paintings of Henry Clay and Isaac Shelby. Lieutenant Governor James E. Cantrill, described by his contemporaries as one of the state's most handsome men, presided over the senate, and during the 1880 session James Blackburn, who resembled Charles Dickens when the novelist was in his prime, was one of the most active senators.

Members of the legislature lived in hotels and rooming houses during their biennial sessions; most of the lawmakers were genuinely interested in the welfare of the state, but there were a few members whose sincerity could be questioned. Occasionally quorums were impossible to obtain, judgments were clouded by liquor, or tempers flared into verbal battles. A reporter for the *Courier-Journal* observed that the "awful strain of three hours daily work" was too much for some legislative brains and criticized those who "sat like knots on logs" sleeping or admiring the ladies in the gallery. A representative from Marion County became so

Old State House, ca. 1900.
Courtesy of Kentucky Library, Western Kentucky University

disgusted with the chicanery of his fellow legislators that he went home at the end of the second week of the 1880 session. Quipped the *Courier-Journal*, "the change of his status" from the "dead sea level of common every day life to the dizzy heights of the Capitoline Olympus" was too much for him.[10] Another, Republican John D. White of Clay County, frequently monopolized the floor of the house to deliver blistering tirades against the governor and other Democrats. He, too, finally resigned, and one of his critics suggested he had made so many enemies during his brief stay in Frankfort that he needed a bodyguard. Apparently, however, his constituents approved of his conduct, for White was elected to Congress in 1881.

The first few days of each legislative session were spent in selecting seats and choosing a speaker for the lower house, doorkeepers for both houses, and a state librarian, positions for which a multitude of candidates campaigned. Seating arrangements for both houses were based on a first-come, first-choice method. A letter to Representative Clarence McElroy of Bowling Green, an unsuccessful candidate for speaker, illustrates the shenanigans that preceded the 1881 session.

The day after the election Tom Harris and Bill Reiley [William Railey of Woodford Co.] went over and selected all of the best seats for their friends. The aisle seats were, of course, gobbled up first, and therefore there is no chance for a seat in either the 3rd or 4th rows. They were kind enough, however, to remember you by placing your name on the seat Gen. Buford occupied when a member, the front seat on the left. Gov. Meriweather [Louisville] is down for your deskmate, Squire Massey [Warren County] has a seat on the right, but not on the aisle. I would certainly have raised a row, if necessary, and gotten the seat you wanted, but thought there was no use, as the general opinion seems to be that you will have no use for a seat on the floor, and if this should prove true, Squire Massey can take your seat and let someone else have his.[11]

Once seating details and elections were out of the way, the General Assembly informed Blackburn it was "duly organized and ready to receive any communications His Excellency might desire to submit." The first such communication was the governor's message, a formal statement of the executive's priorities and official observations. The bulk of Blackburn's 1880 message concerned the need for reforms—fiscal, judicial, educational, and penal. Kentucky lived in a fool's paradise, said Blackburn, having spent since 1867 over three million dollars more than her revenue receipts. The state's finances, he warned, could only get worse, for the war claims received from the federal government, which accounted for most of the three million, were nearly exhausted, taxes had been reduced by the previous legislature, and the depression of the mid-1870s had decreased property values. The answer to the financial dilemma was to increase taxes, reevaluate property, and eliminate the "great frauds" that "robbed the treasury of tens of thousands of dollars," frauds incurred through padded accounts against the state, unnecessary expenses involving trials and the conveyance of prisoners to the state prison, and manufactured claims against the state.[12]

In answer to his request for reforms, the legislature responded with a variety of laws designed to save money. The amount of money saved in the state's annual two-to-three-million-dollar budget was nebulous, but the improvement in the administration of justice was important.

Taxes on real property were increased five cents per one hundred dollars value, and salaries of state officials were reduced by about one-fifth. In addition, laws were strengthened to help state agents collect taxes from individuals and from county sheriffs.

Maximum allotments were set for the care of prisoners and their transportation from one county to another or to the state prison.

Unnecessary court systems were abolished and the circuit court districts were revamped to provide for more efficiency. The pay for circuit court jurors was fixed at one dollar per day for petit jurors and a dollar and a quarter for grand jurors. The number of jurors for police and quarterly courts was reduced to six, and their compensation was set at fifty cents per case or one dollar per day when more than one case was heard. Penalties were established for soliciting service as a juror.

Salaries for judges and prosecuting attorneys were to be established in advance rather than determined by the number of cases heard and convictions won. Finally, because public clamor demanded an end of the barbaric, circuslike affairs, the legislature abolished public executions.

The administration of justice was further aided in 1882 when, at Blackburn's suggestion, the legislation created the Superior Court to relieve the overcrowded docket of the Court of Appeals. Three elected judges whose qualifications were equal to those of the appeals court judges composed the new court. Appellate jurisdiction of the court was limited to cases involving less than $3,000. Judges J. H. Bowden of Russellville, A. E. Richards of Louisville, and Richard Reid of Mount Sterling were elected and performed ably the duties delegated to them. Within a few years the dockets of the two courts were cleared of the tremendous backlog of cases, but the Superior Court was unpopular, for it was regarded as the "poor man's court." It was abolished in 1890.

Another of Blackburn's concerns was for the improvement of river navigation. In the early months of 1879 Congress had appropriated $100,000 for improvements on the Kentucky River, but many Kentuckians believed that federally funded internal improvements were unconstitutional. Blackburn suggested to the 1880 legislature that navigation improvements would aid in the development of untapped riches in coal, timber, and other resources. Since the state could not afford to finance the needed improvements, federal funds should be used. Taxes on Kentucky products, said the governor, had contributed millions of dollars to federal revenues; the appropriation was merely returning to the state some of the money that had been derived from it. Blackburn's argument was convincing, and the legislature approved the use of federal monies. Two years later additional funds were made available for improvements on the Licking, Big Sandy, and Cumberland rivers, and, again, at Blackburn's urging, the legislature approved the use of federal funds.

Believing that "education forms and fashions the character of a state, because it forms and fashions the character of the men and women who constitute the state," Blackburn took a special interest in the development of the Agricultural and Mechanical College, an affiliate of Kentucky University. The school had been torn by a sectarian quarrel during the early part of the decade, and enrollment declined from 200 in 1869 to 66 in 1879. Blackburn suggested to the legislature that the A & M College be reorganized and made "the People's College, a representative institution in its highest and truest sense."[13] The solons concurred. The school's management was vested in a twelve-man board of trustees appointed and presided over by the governor. Scholarships based on competitive examinations were made available to Kentucky students. Lexington offered her city park as a site for the school, Fayette County contributed money for additional land, and Lexington city bonds financed the construction of buildings. The Administration Building of the new University of Kentucky was dedicated in February 1882.

Two of Blackburn's requests to the legislature related to his profession. At his suggestion the state erected a monument at Hickman in memory of the physicians and volunteers who died during the 1878 epidemic. More important than his salute to fallen comrades, however, was his effort to aid the State Board of Health. Blackburn informed the General Assembly that in the late summer of 1878 the president of the State Board of Health had requested that Governor McCreary establish quarantine stations at the state's borders, but "in absence of all laws" enabling him to do so, protective measures were impossible. Many Kentuckians died because such measures were not taken, Blackburn asserted. When the fever reached the commonwealth, the governor "could do nothing more but give of his private purse, which he did liberally," and the president of the board used his personal funds to send nurses to fever-ridden Hickman. Increased powers and appropriations, said Blackburn, would enable the board to "adopt and enforce sanitary measures to protect the lives and property of our citizens. Life is more to be prized than wealth or property. When wealth is lost, it may be regained, but in death all is lost forever."[14] Again, the legislature consented and amended the original Board of Health Bill, increasing its emergency powers. Additional appropriations, however, were not provided until 1882, and then they were meager. A Louisville paper compared the legislature's miserly gesture to that of "giving a man a fine carriage who has no horse."[15]

Blackburn's greatest aid to the State Board of Health was in his appointment of Joseph N. McCormack of Bowling Green as the board's secretary. Serving in that capacity from 1883 to 1922, McCormack fought for legislation that required smallpox vaccinations of all school children and pasteurization of milk and for scores of other laws designed to improve public health. Under his direction the health department eventually became an effective, farsighted organization that worked diligently to educate Kentuckians on matters of life and health.

When the legislature was not in session, some of the governor's activities centered around his duties as commander-in-chief of the state guard. Established in 1878, the guard experienced its first summer training session in the summer of 1880. At Blackburn's suggestion the ten-day encampment was held at Crab Orchard, for it was accessible by rail from all areas of the state and was a healthy location. The choice, however, proved to be a poor one, for "Camp Blackburn" was too far from a water supply and too close to the resort area, which provided "many temptations . . . to engage in social pleasures inconsistent with military duty."[16] Blackburn attended the guard's encampment for several days, although his accommodations were at the resort rather than in the tents with the men, and he reviewed the troops and even rode with the cavalry on one occasion.

In the spring of 1881 Kentucky was invited to be represented at the Yorktown Centennial, and Blackburn reasoned that a battalion of state guards should attend to salute Kentucky's mother-state. Unfortunately, no money was allocated for such activities, and the legislature would not be in session until after the October affair. Several railroads offered to carry Kentucky's troops to Virginia at reduced rates, and Blackburn, who seemed sure that the legislature would reimburse him, signed a note for about $7,000 of the expenses required to send five companies. A few days before the festivities began, the smartly uniformed guards and several state officials, including the governor, made the trip to Yorktown. As the Virginia-bound train passed through Mount Sterling, residents of that town passed out lunch baskets filled with delectable edibles to the travelers.

The troops enjoyed the celebration at Yorktown, and their exemplary conduct received praise from Virginians and their leaders. But in Kentucky the Yorktown visit was severely criticized. Many state residents viewed the entire affair as an unnecessary and expensive "wild goose chase," and the report of Blackburn riding at the head of Virginia troops "like a knight of old . . . [paying] chivalric attention to the old mother state" resulted in many critical editorials.[17] Although a Robertson County newspaper urged the 1881-1882 legislature to appropriate funds to cover the Yorktown expenses and not leave the patriotic governor holding the debt, the solons refused to do so. Monies that accumulated in the guards' encampment fund eventually paid the debt.

Two months after the guards returned from Yorktown, Blackburn called out units from Lexington, Maysville, and Midway to preserve order in Boyd County, where an Ashland mob threatened to lynch a self-admitted rapist and axe-murderer along with his two accomplices in the death of three teenagers. The accused men were taken to Lexington for safekeeping, and then returned to Catlettsburg for trial. Two of them, Ellis Craft and William Neal, were found guilty and sentenced to be executed, but an appeal for a new trial was granted. The third man, George Ellis, received a sentence of life imprisonment. On the evening after his trial, an irate mob removed Ellis from the jail and hanged him from a sycamore tree. Blackburn immediately sent 188 guardsmen back to Boyd County to take the two remaining men to Lexington. As the steamer carrying the guards and their prisoners passed Ashland, fifty to one hundred men aboard a ferryboat fired on the troops, and the guardsmen returned the fire. During the brief battle several bystanders on the riverbank and some of the men on the ferry were killed or wounded, but the steamer proceeded to Maysville. A change of venue was granted for Neal's and Craft's second trial, and Blackburn ordered 416 men to accompany them to Carter County and remain there for the duration of the trial. Although there was no hint of trouble, the encampment in eastern Kentucky in "the most wretched [February] weather—ice, sleet, snow, and mud, in something like equal proportions," severely tested the endurance of the "veteran troops."[18] For his use of the guards to preserve and restore order, Blackburn was a target for both praise and chastisement.

Throughout his administration criticism of Blackburn by many of the state's newspapers was severe. Some would have found fault with any Democrat who held the office, but many small-town papers took delight in stirring up discontent regarding all of the governor's deeds. Papers that earlier seemed unconcerned about the physician's lack of political experience now reprimanded him for his political naïveté. The executive's independence and refusal to follow their wishes infuriated powerful Democrats who had expected the governor to be their stooge. In October 1879 Commissioner of Agriculture C. E. Bowman had observed that Blackburn was "running the government according to his own notions" and predicted that when his four-year term was over "his own footprint will be so clear all along through it that none will dare charge that it was other than Blackburn's administration."[19] The most obvious footprints resulted from Blackburn's determination to aid the inmates at the Kentucky Penitentiary. His method of trying to force the state to assume responsibility for the prison and its inmates incurred the wrath of former friends and foes alike. Uninterested in a political career, Blackburn pushed an issue that would surely have thwarted any such ambition to hold other offices. Many Democrats feared his actions jeopardized their own futures.

5

PRISON REFORMER

Twentieth-century penologists have called Luke Blackburn the "father" of prison reforms in Kentucky, but the crusade to improve conditions at the Kentucky Penitentiary in Frankfort did not originate with Blackburn. Throughout most of the nineteenth century, penitentiary reports sent to the legislature repeatedly lamented the institution's swampy site and mentioned the need for a better-located facility. Early in the 1870s Henry Watterson's editorials urging improvements at the prison appeared from time to time in the *Courier-Journal*. Republican William O. Bradley stressed the need for prison reforms in his 1875 gubernatorial campaign speeches, and Democratic Governor James B. McCreary urged the 1878 legislature to appropriate money for an auxiliary prison to alleviate the overcrowded Frankfort institution. Although the lawmakers debated the issue, they adjourned in the spring of 1878 without providing a solution for any of the prison's problems. Therefore, the Louisville paper stepped up its campaign with vivid descriptions of abominable conditions at the seventy-eight-year-old institution. Blackburn undoubtedly read with horror Watterson's accounts of the dilapidated prison that held half again as many convicts as it was meant to house, of the stench caused by filth, and of the high death rate among prisoners. Kentucky's "Black Hole of Calcutta," as it had earlier been dubbed by Bradley, attracted the attention of concerned citizens, who denounced former legislators for refusing to rectify the disgrace of long standing.

The state's first major penal code reform occurred in 1798 with the legislature's creation of the penitentiary and reduction of the number of capital offenses. Built on an acre of swampy land donated by Harry Innes, the prison opened for use in 1800 as a place where lawbreakers could be punished by confinement and hard labor. Through the years additional marshy acreage was added, and by 1879 the prison's twenty-two-foot-high walls encompassed about five acres. The poorly drained and debris-filled quadrangle contained a chapel and hospital building, a two-story workshop, a three-story hemp house, a five-tier cell house for men, a small two-story house that accommodated thirty-two women, and a variety of unsightly shacks used as smokehouses, bathhouse, latrine, and hemp hackling sheds. The large cell house enclosed 744 cells, each measuring less than seven by four by seven feet. Nine hundred and seventy men lived in these poorly ventilated, inadequately heated, and filthy quarters. The prison yard's open sewers, which had insufficient fall to carry off the filth to the nearby Kentucky River, overflowed in the rainy season; in the dry season the filth accumulated. The noxious odor emanating from the privy and sewers could be detected for several blocks.

The prison's death rate, always high, set a record in 1879. Newspapers reported exaggerated daily death counts during that spring and summer, but the prison's physician recorded seventy-five mortalities, over half of which were due to pneumonia and tuberculosis. In June 1879 scurvy appeared at the penitentiary. More than two hundred men suffering with it were confined to the hospital, and "God only knows how many prisoners were still at work" with the malady.[1]

Throughout most of its history the penitentiary was operated by a keeper or lessee who rented the institution and its inhabitants from the state and had complete control over them. The lessee, who was chosen by the legislature, fed, clothed, and provided bedding for the prisoners; he also hired guards and maintained order. The prisoners worked

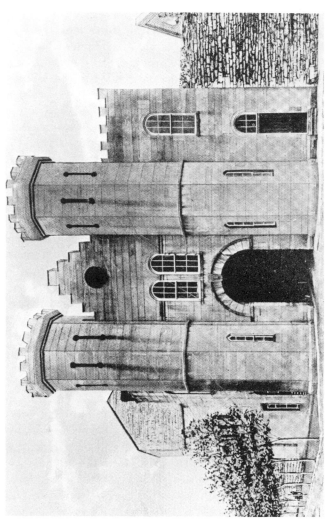

Gate of the Kentucky Penitentiary, ca. 1900.
Courtesy of Kentucky Library, Western Kentucky University

at a variety of tasks, including the production of hemp rope and bagging, chairs, tables, and various other household items. Profits from their labors paid for food, supplies, and general prison maintenance; the net gains belonged to the lessee, who increased his profits by cutting corners on necessities and by neglecting to keep the buildings and grounds in good condition. Operating a prison was a lucrative business, and money and favors passed between candidates for the position and members of the legislature every four years at lessee-selection time. In 1879 Jeremiah South began his fourth term as lessee. A native of eastern Kentucky and a member of the Democratic State Central Committee, the sixty-eight-year-old "Colonel" South enjoyed great popularity with the legislators, for he generously supplied them with cheap board, including free laundry and drinks, and presented to them walking sticks, cedar chests, and other prison-made items. Because of his influence, earlier lawmakers had rejected reforms opposed by South.

Following his nomination for governor, Blackburn spent considerable time reading publications on prison management. By inaugural day he was unusually well versed on the American prison system. A few days after his inauguration Blackburn announced that the affairs of the state prison would be his chief interest and major subject when he addressed the legislature in early January, but until the General Assembly convened, his only recourse was to aid the overcrowded institution by executive clemency. His pardoning power, the new governor promised, would be used in the interest of humanity and would be governed by his sense of justice.

His first pardon, granted the day after his inauguration, was for a Shelby County official sentenced but not yet incarcerated for intoxication. Five days later he granted pardons to seven inmates whose poor health and enfeebled condition touched his heart. One of the men was a Pendleton County resident serving six years for Ku Kluxing and robbery, but now nearly dead with scurvy. This convict's release set off the first of many bitter denunciations of the governor's pardoning policy. A large group of citizens met at the Pendleton County Courthouse and censured the governor for releasing a man whom no one wanted returned to the community—a man with a long record of violent deeds. The *Falmouth Independence* questioned not only the governor's decision but also his diagnosis, for the man who was supposedly near death managed to return home unattended. To the chastisement Blackburn responded that no "little eight-by-ten backwoods newspaper would deter him from doing what was right."[2] The *Hickman Courier* warned the new official not to forget that these county papers were responsible for his election, and the *Paducah Daily News* suggested that a man "should never abuse the bridge over which he passes in safety."[3] By the time the legislature convened in late December, Blackburn had pardoned fifty-two men and boys confined to the prison. Criticisms of his "abuse" of the executive privilege radiated from every part of the state.

A sizable portion of Blackburn's address to the 1880 legislature concerned the Frankfort institution. Admitting that he felt "the blush of shame" for accumulated horrors at the state's "great college and university of crime," the governor described the facility in vivid terms. He also discussed at some length the progressive ideas of contemporary prison reformers and made constructive suggestions for the improved care of the state's wards. He urged the legislature to abolish the barbaric leasing system and adopt the warden system, to employ a physician and pay him a salary sufficient to enable him to devote his entire attention to the prison's medical and health problems, to increase the monetary limits of petty larceny so that minor offenders could be committed to county jails and workhouses rather than to the Frankfort prison, and to appropriate money for the creation of another prison. Denouncing the archaic penitentiary system sanctioned by the laws of Kentucky, Blackburn urged the General Assembly to "abandon a policy which is based on abasement and cruelty, and whose only marks are degradation from the moment the wretched convict dons his striped zebra suit, until he emerges from the prison with hope forever blasted and manhood forever crushed."[4]

In response to Blackburn's plea the house appointed a committee of five legislators, including three physicians, to inspect the penitentiary and report its findings. The grim report, delivered on January 19, 1880, told of prisoners confined to the hospital who could live no more than a few months, and of others who would be dead by spring; of more than 200 inmates unfit for work; of poorly drained grounds that caused a "malaria rendering the atmosphere impure and tending to induce diseases of the lungs"; of accumulated filth on the grounds and lack of cleanliness in the overcrowded cell houses and workshops; of malfunctioning ventilating systems and insufficient and unwholesome food. The committee urged the governor to pardon at least eight men who were almost dead.[5] Shocked by what they heard, the solons selected another committee, composed of the nine doctors in both houses of the legislature, who met with Blackburn the following day and toured the prison. During their visit they compiled a list of sixty-nine men and boys who should be released. A few days later the governor pardoned eighty-four ill or youthful inmates.

A later and more extensive investigation, conducted by a committee of the senate, attempted to find out not only what were the conditions at the Black Hole, but also how they came to be that way. The senate committee questioned about thirty witnesses, whose testimonies were included in the findings returned to a joint session of the General Assembly. Delivering the report in late February before a gallery filled with visitors, the committee emphasized conditions that Blackburn had stressed earlier and that had been discussed in the newspapers from time to time for several years. What should have been common knowledge suddenly joggled the consciences of the legislators. The report was vague yet shocking; the testimony of the witnesses was terrifying. Among other unsavory details, the legislature learned of these conditions:

The unheated bathhouse contained only two large tubs, in which three or four persons bathed simultaneously. Ten to twelve men washed in the same dirty water. Convicts were encouraged to bathe weekly, but few washed that often.

The prisoners ate an inadequate and unwholesome diet. Heavy clammy cornbread that "smelled like fermented Indian meal," salted meat, and scorched and unsweetened "coffee" made from chicory were the diet mainstays. Several witnesses suggested that the prison purchased rancid, even putrid, meat, and an area farmer swore that a two-day-old carcass lying in his field was skinned and taken to the prison kitchen. Several witnesses debated the cause of the scurvy outbreak. One doctor testified that lack of vegetables caused scurvy, but another physician claimed overcrowding caused the malady. The lessee and his assistant insisted that the general diet was wholesome and contained sufficient vegetables. A Franklin County farmer, who believed he reinforced South's claim about sufficient vegetables, quoted from his records of foods he ordered sent to the prison kitchen for the year ending October 1, 1879: 2,205 bushels of potatoes, 9,141 heads of cabbage, 298 bushels of greens, 415 bushels of turnips, 47 bushels of tomatoes, 187 bushels of green beans, 392 loads of squash, 54,386 pounds of beef. A kitchen employee claimed that some of the meat received at the prison was tainted and was therefore made into soap and that many of the vegetables were rotten and were fed to the hogs. When questioned on the quantity needed for a meal, he replied that nine bushels of potatoes and seventy-five heads of cabbage made a "mess" for 1,000 men.

Inmates answered evening roll call in the uncovered prison yard. Their rain-soaked clothing frequently froze in the unheated cell house during the winter night, but they wore the stiff garments the following morning, for extras were unavailable. Opinion was divided on the adequacy of the clothing issued to inmates. The prison did not supply the men with underwear, but each convict received two cotton shirts, a pair of pants, and a denim jacket. Shirts were laundered once a week; pants and jackets were worn for several months between washings.

Bedding consisted of a ticking mattress filled with Spanish moss or straw, two or more cotton blankets, and a comforter.

Most of the men worked in the unheated, unventilated hemp department, where the dust was so thick it was impossible to recognize a man at twenty feet. Hence, frostbite and respiratory diseases were commonplace among hemp workers.

Punishment for infractions of prison rules varied and was inconsistent. Confinement in the cell on Sunday and whippings on the bare skin with a leather strap were the most frequently used measures. One witness testified that he saw a convict, who stole clothing from a prison guard, receive 150 lashes, but the institution's officials denied ever administering more than 15 or 20 lashes. No records of offenses or punishments were kept.

The main cell house had defective ventilating and heating equipment. A Louisville architect studied the structure and machinery and stated that "it would be scarcely possible by any machinery to render the cells healthy and safe if they all were occupied." He also noted that the use of wooden night buckets in the cells and the convicts' aversion to bathing "very materially affects the atmosphere."

South and the guards slaughtered cattle in the quadrangle for their friends in Frankfort. The offal from this activity, dumped into the prison's sewers, compounded the stench that permeated the area.

Forcing male convicts to sleep double in the cells and allowing "all grades and ages of men too free and promiscuous intercourse" encouraged widespread practice of sodomy. Twenty percent of the convicts confined to the penitentiary were less than twenty-one years of age.[6]

The witnesses venomously refuted every conclusion drawn by the investigators, but some of them based their knowledge on hearsay, especially on information derived from prison guards and officials. Apparently this was how previous investigations of complaints had been conducted. The committee did not question prisoners or former convicts.

Certainly the lack of administrative leadership contributed to the prison's horrors. Lessee South, ill for several years, permitted his son Sam to operate the prison, and the son allowed assistants and even inmate-trustees a wide range of unsupervised authority. Some of South's friends in the senate tried to transfer a portion of the blame for the prison's horrors to the assistant lessee, to the guards, and even to former Governor McCreary. McCreary told the committee he visited the prison "tolerably often," and his assistant secretary of state, who checked the facility for him occasionally, had assured him that the food and clothing were adequate and the treatment of the prisoners was proper. A Frankfort newspaper quipped that the assistant's reports to McCreary made the penitentiary "sound like the Galt House or the Grand Hotel."[7]

The prison, it seemed, had always been considered a necessary evil in which no one had enough interest to investigate properly reports of wrongdoing or inadequate facilities. Even well-intentioned persons apparently thought that substandard food, inadequate shelter, abominable working conditions, and personal filth were good enough for malefactors. After all, many law-abiding citizens lived and worked under similar conditions.

Repulsed by what they discovered about the penitentiary, yet wishing to absolve South from blame, the senate committee members suggested the removal of the assistant keeper. When the report was read before the General Assembly, however, the house was less charitable toward the lessee. The governor, its members agreed, should remove Jerry South from office immediately. South's friends in both houses argued that his contract with the state did not expire until 1883 and could not be broken by the executive. He could only be impeached by the house and removed by the senate, an unlikely action in view of the lessee's popularity and political influence. The suggestion for his removal was tabled, and all chances for reform might have ended had not Blackburn continued his prodding.

Throughout February and March the governor encouraged action with his unorthodox attendance at many of the legislature's debates. He listened attentively from the visitors' gallery as the lawmakers discussed the pros and cons of his proposed warden system, the advisability of removing South, and the available options by which the prison could be relieved of its overflowing population. The branch penitentiary which Blackburn advocated could have no immediate effect on the Frankfort facility. The overcrowded prison could be relieved by hiring out convicts to work on public projects, but objections were raised because the use of convicts eliminated jobs otherwise available to free laborers. Each house rejected bills passed by the other, and important legislation was lost as the State House filled with heated and empty oratory.

As the legislature investigated, resolved, argued, and postponed action, convicts sickened and the governor issued pardons. Newspapers across the state stepped up their derision of the wrangling legislators and praised—or damned— the governor for his pardons. Residents of towns to which the "cut throats and thieves" returned feared for their safety and claimed that newly pardoned convicts elevated the crime and unemployment rates. A Cincinnati paper poked fun at the feuding legislators by suggesting that if they delayed long enough, "all of the thieves and murderers . . . will be dead. There won't be a wicked man left in Kaintuck."[8] The *Courier-Journal* hounded the legislature for action and praised Blackburn's efforts to make the solons act. The commonwealth, said Watterson's paper, should "congratulate itself on having an executive who knows his duty and dares to do it." The governor's niece also applauded "the man who dares to do right—who courts not public opinion" and published in the Louisville paper a poem about his efforts to aid the prison.[9]

Hampered by their loyalties to South and by their constituents' opposition to increased expenditures and potential loss of employment, the members of the General Assembly were in an understandable bind, but a solution to the problem involving South came in an unexpected manner. Anxious to clear his name from accusations of neglect and mismanagement, South's admirers encouraged the lessee to appear before the Frankfort lawmakers and defend himself. Leaving his sickbed, to which he had been confined for more than a month, South visited the capitol on the morning of April 14 and was enthusiastically greeted by his friends. While discussing with a group of intimates the accusations that "hounded him half to death," South suddenly gasped for breath and went limp. By the time one of the physician-legislators reached South, he was dead. The confusion resulting from the shocking event increased with the hysterical cries of his daughter: "They have killed him with their talk of impeachment and removal. They have murdered our poor dear father."[10] On Senator James Blackburn's suggestion, both houses immediately adjourned until after South's funeral, one of the largest ever held in Frankfort. While the flag flew at half-mast over the capitol, his friends hailed South as a noble man and one of the state's greatest philanthropists.

When the legislators returned to their chambers five days later, the problem of the lessee and his contract no longer existed. Either a new lessee or a new warden had to be chosen, and most of the lawmakers knew the voters favored the warden system. Blackburn appointed South's son to supervise the prison until other arrangements could be made, and while state offices overflowed with greedy candidates for whatever position the legislature created, the penitentiary problem received serious consideration. During the remainder of April the suggestions Blackburn had proposed in his January address were written into laws. A few days before adjournment, the legislature sent to the governor two bills that he quickly signed. One ended the lessee system; the other provided immediate and long-range plans for relieving the overcrowded penitentiary. Because of Blackburn's prodding, the 1880 legislature had set forth the first major reforms in more than twenty years.

Act 1377 provided for the government, management, and discipline of the Kentucky Penitentiary. A salaried warden, elected to a four-year term by a joint ballot of the house and senate, took charge of the prison and its inhabitants. His carefully defined supervisory and administrative duties included: providing strict discipline; arranging useful labor for the convicts, from which he should receive no pecuniary profits; supervising the efforts of all other officers of the prison; examining daily the health, diet, comfort, and safety of the inmates; contracting and purchasing raw materials needed by the facility; hiring assistants and guards as necessary; and reporting monthly the financial state of the prison. The governor, secretary of state, attorney general, and auditor served as the commissioners or directors of the prison. Their powers included the selection of a full-time deputy warden, physician, and clerk, and a part-time chaplain. The act also instructed the prison directors, jointly and individually, to visit the prison at least once a month, and to hire out to a contractor the labors of all the convicts.

Act 1378 provided for the relief of the overcrowding at the prison. A committee of three, appointed by the governor and approved by the senate, was to study existing prison systems in the eastern portion of the nation and select a site for Kentucky's proposed branch penitentiary. To relieve the Frankfort prison until the opening of a new one, and to conform to the prevailing idea that convicts should pay their expenses and net a profit for the state, the act authorized the prison directors to contract the labors of all convicts in excess of 600 upon public works within the state. No prisoner serving more than five years or confined for murder, rape, attempted rape, or arson was eligible to work outside the prison, and no malefactor could labor within the corporate limits of a town, or be quartered within two miles of a town or within one-fourth mile of a private residence. The contractor who hired the convicts also fed, clothed, housed, and guarded them and provided medical care for the sick and injured.

The contract system was little better than the old lessee system, but to gain the branch penitentiary and alleviate the overcrowded conditions in the penitentiary, Blackburn accepted it. The branch penitentiary was an unpopular idea with many of the legislators and a large segment of the populace; spending the taxpayers' money on criminals was not politically expedient. Nevertheless, the legislature included the provision for the branch penitentiary as a means of gaining the governor's signature on the bills.

With the prison bills signed, changes commenced at the Kentucky Penitentiary. The General Assembly selected William S. Stone of Owensboro as warden, despite opposition from the prison directors. Stone's major qualification for the position was his friendship with South's supporters. As an administrator Stone was little better than Jerry South, but his authority was considerably diminished from that of the lessee. Although candidates for other positions appeared as rapidly as "frog-stools after a rain," ability rather than political influence was the major criterion for the choices made by the prison directors.[11] For clerk they selected L. D. Holloway. One of Morgan's raiders during the war, Holloway had spent several months in a northern military prison and thus had some understanding of a prisoner's plight. Thomas South, a son of the former lessee, became deputy warden; on South's death in January of 1882 Harry I. Todd was made deputy warden. Dr. Daniel Gober, who served with Blackburn at Hickman, accepted an appointment as prison physician, and the Reverend J. B. Tharp, a Frankfort minister and teacher, became the chaplain.

Stone and the other officials assumed formal control of the prison June 1, 1880. They and the directors drew up rules and regulations for the government of the penitentiary, and a few months later the directors awarded contracts for the inmates' labors. The contractor in charge of the prison workshops agreed to pay the state $25,000 per year; in return he received the services of 500-600 convicts and the use of the prison's facilities. Each convict took an assigned job and met a daily quota—twenty-five chair frames, two whiskey barrels, twelve flour barrels, or a prescribed number of yards of hemp fabric—or was punished. The majority of the felons worked in the hemp house, where the choking dust irritated eyes and throats and caused a variety of pulmonary and respiratory disorders. The daily output expected of the hemp workers supposedly corresponded to that of free laborers who toiled in hemp factories across the state, but the convicts believed their assignments unreasonable and expressed their hatred for the "living death" with acts of self-mutilation. The prison physician recorded within a two-year period that three men chopped off their hands with hatchets, five cut off one or more fingers, and two slashed their arms to escape the hemp house. A former convict told a Louisville reporter of his experiences in the hemp rooms and said he prayed that "God [would] wither the arms that built that room."[12] Three hundred or more of the healthiest convicts worked on railroads and other public works. The contractors supplied all their needs and paid the state fifty dollars per year per man. The commonwealth hired an inspector to visit the railroad camps periodically and see that the contractors fulfilled their obligations to the prisoners.

The departure of several hundred convicts for the railroad camps in the autumn of 1880 alleviated the overcrowding at the penitentiary. If all went smoothly under the new system, the state could expect to make an annual profit of $17,000 or more on the prisoners. But the contractors did not pay as promised, and when the state pressed them to fulfill their obligations, they threatened to renege on the agreements, which would force the state to assume all responsibility and expense for the care of the convicts. The contractor rather than the warden wielded the power under the new system.

Warden Stone assumed his duties with the air of a man who intended to rectify past injuries. His improvements in the prison's physical plant included the installation of a new heating apparatus for the cell houses, workshops, and hospital kitchen; the cleaning and grading of the prison yard; and the removal of the unsightly hemp hackling sheds. In his November 1881 report to the legislature, Stone described in detail his crude but sincere attempt to put the cell house "in perfect order so far as cleanliness is concerned."

The cell house I found infected with all kinds of vermin known to institutions of this kind, and which I proceeded to remedy. This was done by thoroughly scraping the whitewashed walls with iron scrapers made of tobacco knives with curved handles. The floor, badly rat-eaten, was taken up and the vacuum filled with clay well pounded, and raised two inches above the door sills. Planks were put down *solid* so as to leave no room for incubation. They were then covered with shavings and hemp herds, sprinkled well with coal oil from watering cans. The walls, ceilings, and iron bedsteads were likewise treated, and the whole set on fire, which completely destroyed insects and eggs. I then coal-tarred the iron doors instead of whitewashing, and found the odor a preventive to the approach of these pests. I then proceeded to fill all the cracks and crevices with mortar and covered the whole with a coat of thin whitewash. This has been done three times during the present summer, and the cells are now as free of vermin as it is possible to get them.[13]

Despite these efforts prisoners continued to complain of the handfuls of bugs that shared their beds and of the general filth of the cell house.

In his relations with the contractor and other prison officials, Stone lacked finesse. He interfered with the contractor's work requirements, and the contractor complained that Stone encouraged laziness among the convicts. Complaints were also levied about Stone's severe punishments, although his reports to the prison directors and the legislature insisted that he favored "humane treatment and kindly words" and was following in "the footsteps of that good and much lamented citizen, Col. Jerry South . . . whose acts of gentleness, generosity and philanthropy are well remembered by those who knew him."[14] In the late fall of 1881

Stone embarrassed the state by his arrest in Cincinnati for assaulting a young hotel clerk in a dispute over a hotel bill. The combination of this embarrassment, the bickering with the contractor, and the complaints of severe punishment resulted in an investigation into Stone's actions by the governor, prison physician, and a committee of the legislators. Although their report castigated Stone's severity, the lethargic lawmakers refused to reprimand the warden. Pressure exerted by Blackburn and other prison directors during the summer of 1882, however, forced Stone's resignation from the position he labeled "an arduous one, involving a change in the entire prison system, imposing duties at once novel and responsible."[15] The directors appointed Harry I. Todd to fill Stone's unexpired term. Todd was a cut above South and Stone. Although his record of punishments included ordering twenty stripes for a prisoner who repeatedly gambled and swore, Todd's discipline generated few complaints. His cooperation with the contractors and prison directors encouraged a relatively smooth-running prison, and his efforts to provide competent guards impressed the directors. Todd requested a raise in the forty- to fifty-dollar-weekly salaries for prison guards, who worked a ninety-hour week. Good men were hard to find and keep, and higher salaries and a graduated pay scale, Todd suggested, could be used as an incentive to capable men. He also suggested that "subordinate positions should be used as a training school for our wardens and deputy wardens," an idea the directors echoed in their report to the legislature.[16]

Todd also made numerous physical improvements during his brief wardenship. The prison wall and many of the brick buildings were pointed up and repaired, the wells and cisterns were cleaned, the sewers and gutters in the prison yard were rebuilt to provide a better slope for drainage, and a bathroom containing twenty-four tubs and an overhead sprinkler supplying steam-heated water was built on the first floor of the main cell house. Todd was much concerned about the niggardly supply of bedding provided for the convicts, and shortly after Blackburn left office Todd complained to the contractor that the shortage of these items was so acute that the arrival of a few new convicts would necessitate the redistribution of bedding, for there were no extra blankets or mattresses. The contractor replied that sufficient bedding had been sent to the prison; to request more made "extraordinary demands . . . upon us."[17] Despite his efficient administration of the prison, the 1884 legislature replaced Todd with another of the former lessee's sons, Barry South, whom Todd labeled an incompetent and an "utter failure in all his business dealings."[18] South's attempt to supplant Todd's guards with his own friends was bitterly opposed by the prison directors and flared into a power struggle between them and the legislature. Under the prodding of Governor J. Proctor Knott, Blackburn's successor, the legislature dismissed South and appointed a warden acceptable to the directors. The independent power of the warden ended.

The inmates' most effective friend was the prison physician, Daniel Gober, who believed that a doctor's first duty was to prevent disease and sickness. Shortly after his appointment he ordered the construction of a covered passageway between the cell house and the dining room, for he reasoned that wearing wet clothing increased the prisoners' susceptibility to respiratory illnesses. Gober also insisted on wholesome food. The inmates were fed on ten cents per day, an adequate amount, Gober believed, if his recommended diet was followed:

Breakfast: fried bacon or baked meat, hominy, rice or potatoes, gravy, coffee and cornbread.

Dinner: boiled pork five days a week, boiled and roasted beef the other two days; vegetable soup, and vegetables (kraut, greens or potatoes), coffee, and cornbread.

Supper: light bread, molasses, cold meat, buttermilk.[19]

Gober's instructions were not always obeyed. He complained loudly and frequently that the quality of the food served to prisoners deteriorated when the legislature was not in session—the supply of vegetables diminished, while the amount of salted, fatty pork and bad molasses, which "cause more sickness than anything else," increased.[20] Gober's recommended diet may sound monotonous, but the meals were prepared from relatively wholesome ingredients and contained enough vegetables to prevent scurvy. His frequent visits to the kitchen to inspect the food purchased by the contractor and his occasional supervision of food preparation resulted in a significant reduction in the number of intestinal ailments suffered by the prisoners.

Gober spent most of his time caring for the sick convicts at the prison hospital, and he frequently sent notes to the governor requesting pardons for inmates suffering from incurable or chronic diseases. A few of his pardon requests were for women prisoners, whose clandestine meetings with male inmates or prison employees resulted in pregnancy; Gober believed that babies should have an opportunity to start life in better surroundings than the state penitentiary. Always vocal about injustices he saw, Gober constantly complained to the governor about punishments administered by Warden Stone and the contractor, and he talked freely to newspaper reporters about poor food, unhealthy conditions in the hemp houses, and other prison shortcomings over which he had no control but which he nevertheless believed should be erased.

In the Reverend Tharp, the inmates also had a compassionate friend. On assuming his part-time duties Tharp found the chapel in a distressing condition, for it had been used for many years as a storage room for lumber. Unable to gain cooperation from the warden or contractor, Tharp appealed for help from the governor, who ordered that the chapel be cleaned and used "strictly and solely" for religious and educational activities.[21] The lumber was removed, and Tharp, aided by several convalescing hospital inmates, cleaned, repaired, and repainted the chapel and its meager furnishings, varnished the wooden benches, and built a pul-

Prisoners returning from religious services.

From William C. Sneed, *A Report on the History . . . of the Kentucky Penitentiary . . .* (Frankfort, Ky., 1860)

pit. Tharp held separate services every Sunday morning for male and female inmates, and he invited ministers from Frankfort's various denominations to conduct additional services and hold communion. With donations from friends in Frankfort, Tharp purchased a cabinet organ for the chapel and then organized a choir; the "singing was wonderful," Mrs. Blackburn later declared.[22]

Tharp also tried to organize Sunday afternoon religion classes, but the prisoners did not respond to the convict teachers who helped in this undertaking, and the classes were abandoned. Then in the summer of 1881 Mrs. Blackburn organized Sunday school classes for the inmates, and with the help of the governor's sister, Mary Morris, and several of their friends, the ladies turned what was once the "longest day of the week" into "the sweetest . . . [that] passes only too quickly."[23]

In- and out-of-state newspapers lauded the first lady's activities, those she performed every Sunday and the annual Christmas dinners she and her friends personally prepared for the convicts. The *St. Louis Republican* told its readers of her efforts and suggested that the governors' wives of all the states and territories in the nation should follow Mrs. Blackburn's example and obey the words of Christ: "I was in prison and sick and ye visited me."[24]

Although Chaplain Tharp spent only a few hours each week at the penitentiary, he instituted major improvements in the prison's library. Most of the books were old ones "no intelligent person would want to read," but he nevertheless cataloged and shelved them in bookcases he found in the chapel.[25] He also inserted ads in local newspapers to publicize the need for more reading material. Donations, mostly religious tracts, were sent by missionary societies and church groups, and with the aid of Mrs. Blackburn, who was quite successful in her pleas for money and donations from publishers, booksellers, and individuals, the library's holdings increased from a few hundred dilapidated volumes to several thousand books and pamphlets. Tharp set up a lending system and permitted inmates to borrow two books every two weeks. During the first eighteen months of Tharp's association with the prison, three thousand books circulated, although nearly one-half of the inmates were illiterate.

A teacher by profession, Tharp worked with prisoners who wished to learn to read or to increase their reading skills, and he appealed to the legislature and prison directors to provide slates, textbooks, and primers for the classes he planned to conduct during the convicts' free time. The directors had no money to give, and the legislature remained deaf to his plea. In the summer of 1883 Tharp resigned from his prison post and H. H. Kavanaugh replaced him as a full-time chaplain and teacher. At Kavanaugh's request, the legislature appropriated enough money to provide each convict with a Bible, but funds for textbooks were not made available. Nevertheless, Kavanaugh conducted daily classes in basic reading, writing, English grammar, and practical arithmetic.

In June of 1882 evangelist W. O. Barnes conducted revival meetings in Frankfort. His services at the penitentiary attracted not only most of the inmates but also prison and state officials, including the governor and his wife (Barnes described them as a "dear benevolent-looking old man" and "a very pleasant lady"). Mrs. Blackburn learned that several felons were unable to attend one of the meetings, for they were "loaded down with chains" and locked in their cells for "insubordination and attempting to set fire to the hemp room."[26] Undaunted by possible danger to her person, Julia went to their cells and led them, in their shackles, to the revival service. After Barnes completed his sermon, he invited the members of his audience to confess their sins and come forward to the "mercy seat" and be saved. Among the three hundred convicts who answered his invitation were several in chains. Barnes recorded in his diary: "I never had a deeper joy than in taking these crime-stained hands in mine, and looking into eyes from which all traces of their hard life had vanished, and the expression was, almost without exception, that of feminine softness." At Barnes's revival meet-

98

ing a few days later the "dear old governor made a bold confession, and was the first man to go forward."[27] Three weeks later Blackburn joined the Episcopal Church.

Although conditions improved for those convicts remaining within the penitentiary's walls, the plight of several hundred hired out to railroad contractors was perhaps worse than it had been in the overcrowded pre-1880 facility. Rumors of inhumane treatment, severe beatings, and deaths from accident and exposure compelled Blackburn and Gober in the spring of 1882 to initiate an investigation of conditions at several camps, including those near Boonesborough and Winchester. Three members of each house accompanied the governor and prison physician on the tour, and their report to the General Assembly insisted that the system of hiring out convicts "merits severe condemnation."[28]

Conditions at the various camps differed, but in all camps the insufficiently clad men lived in wooden shacks that were cold in the winter and unbearably hot in the summer. The windows, eight-by-four-inch slits, contained neither glass nor shutters to keep out the wind and rain. Bunks were covered with straw or corn-husk mattresses and thin, dirty blankets. Bathing facilities included a half-barrel of water and a tin basin, but neither soap nor towel was furnished, and no provisions were made to relieve the men of the lice and bedbugs that plagued them.

The investigators found that the food served to prisoners was generally "wholesome" but insufficient in quantity; most of the convicts complained of perpetual hunger. The men ate from wooden bowls and tin cups; flatware was unavailable. Many of the men worked in tunnels, which the investigators found so stifling they were forced to leave after a few minutes. Nevertheless, prisoners labored all day in the airless shafts, standing knee-deep in mud and water, regardless of the temperature. The law which limited the convicts to a ten-hour working day during the summer months and eight hours in the winter was outrageously violated. The contractor insisted that most of the convicts volunteered to work four to six additional hours every day. The law stated that convicts must be paid one dollar per day or twelve-and-a-half cents per hour for their labors, but the investigators found that the prisoners were "defrauded at every turn."[29]

Sickness and injuries plagued the convict railroad crews. The hospital, usually a drafty wooden shanty, was crowded with patients who suffered from pneumonia, fevers, various intestinal and pulmonary disorders, bruises, and broken bones and lay on beds devoid of sheets or pillows, covered only with thin, dirty blankets. Many of their maladies resulted from cruel and frequent punishments. No one person meted out corrective measures; consequently, anyone could vent his anger and call it discipline for a real or imaginary infraction. Whippings with leather straps and beatings with a swab stick were the most frequently used methods of punishing erring felons. The guards, paid by the state and employed to prevent mistreatment, insisted that the men enjoyed adequate care and the same quality of food, housing, and medical service as provided for hired crews. Nevertheless, every convict interviewed by the investigating committee offered to have his sentence doubled or even tripled if he could return to the penitentiary.

In their report to the General Assembly the investigators recommended an "immediate repeal of the law establishing the leasing system; that the contracts with the lessee, violated in every particular, be immediately annulled, and the convicts withdrawn. This civilization and humanity alike demand."[30] The lawmakers shelved the report and made no attempt to improve the plight of the railroad prison gangs, for there was no room at the penitentiary for them, and the state could ill afford to feed and clothe them. As their only effort, the solons suggested that the number of convicts sent to the penitentiary could be reduced by reinstituting the whipping post as a place to punish minor infractions. The whipping post bill was defeated by a narrow margin.

Residents of areas where convicts worked also voiced complaints. In the summer of 1882 Frankfort residents discovered convict laborers repairing the bridge over the Ken-

Inmate of the Kentucky Penitentiary.
From William C. Sneed, *A Report on the
History . . . of the Kentucky Penitentiary . . .*
(Frankfort, Ky., 1860)

tucky River. A group of local citizens drew up a petition in which they stated that the use of convicts on railroads and turnpikes "has grown into an abuse which is unjust to the working man . . . and in violation of the spirit and letter of the law."[31] The petition, sent to Blackburn, requested that the competition with free labor cease and that all convicts be returned to the prison. The governor was powerless to do any more than remind the contractor that the law forbade the use of convicts on public works within the corporate limits of a town.

Blackburn inspected the railroad camps again three months before he left office and again labeled as pernicious the system of leasing out convicts. Powerless to correct the abuses he saw then and on other inspection tours, the governor told a newspaper reporter that he could only help a convict escape ill-treatment by granting him a pardon. The real solution, said Blackburn, was a branch penitentiary where reform rather than punishment was the goal of prison officials.

Despite the changes resulting from Blackburn's efforts, conditions at the penitentiary deteriorated under governors less interested in the plight of society's forgotten men. Throughout the remainder of the nineteenth and during the first three decades of the twentieth centuries, everyone seemed to agree that the prison's low, swampy location was a major drawback to improvements in its physical plant and that the penitentiary should be closed. Nevertheless, it remained in use and was enlarged to house as many as twenty-five hundred inmates. When the waters of the Kentucky River filled the prison's buildings during the great flood of 1937, Governor A. B. Chandler ordered that the inmates be evacuated and that Kentucky's "Black Hole" be closed forever.

6

LENIENT LUKE

Aᴌᴛʜᴏᴜɢʜ ɪᴍᴘʀᴏᴠᴇᴍᴇɴᴛs at the Kentucky Penitentiary were Blackburn's immediate goal, his major interest centered around a plan for beginning a system of small branch
penitentiaries or reformatories using the Irish System of
prison administration. Blackburn compared the Irish System to Christ's teachings of forgiveness based on reformation and repentance rather than on vengeance. The object
of penal discipline, the governor thought, should be the prevention of crime and the salvation of the offender. Blackburn knew that Kentucky's system, more than that of any
other state, brutalized and degraded its wards.

In his addresses to the legislature Blackburn urged the
lawmakers to consider the purpose of prisons, the cause of
crime, and the state's duty to convicts and free citizens.
Quoting from a speech made by former presidential candidate and governor of New York, Horatio Seymour, Blackburn informed the 1880 legislature that "prisoners are men
like ourselves, and if we would learn the dangers which lurk
in our pathways, we must learn how they stumbled and
fell." In reviewing the records of New York's convicts,
Blackburn told his listeners, Seymour recalled not a single
case "where I do not feel that I might have fallen as my fellowman has done if I had been subjected to the same demoralizing influences and pressed by the same temptations."
The Kentucky governor urged the state to build several

small prisons where the object would be to "teach and train the prisoner in such a manner that on his discharge, he may be able to resist temptation and inclined to lead an upright and worthy life."[1]

The Irish System, which Blackburn praised in his addresses to the 1880 and 1881-1882 legislatures consisted of three or more plateaus of treatment. In the first level, to which all new convicts were temporarily committed, the prisoner experienced solitary confinement and hard labor. Through good conduct, obedience to prison rules, and repentance he earned admittance to the second level. There he labored on public works and received religious training and schooling "from those competent and trained to teach him." As his reformation progressed, the inmate received enlarged privileges, learned a trade, and earned money that would be "placed to his credit." Under the multilevel Irish System the prisoner would be reformed and ready to return to society by the end of his term. For those who had difficulties in finding jobs or adjusting to the outside world, Blackburn recommended a new idea that had been introduced in Sweden—special boardinghouses for newly freed convicts who needed shelter and additional guidance.[2]

By replacing the unhealthy, overcrowded facility at Frankfort with numerous small prisons across the state, the governor said, reformation could be aided further by the separation of "young boy culprits . . . from the old and hardened offenders, and those who slew their fellows in sudden heat and passion from cold-blooded and deliberate assassins."[3] In response to Blackburn's plea, and to the adverse publicity about the Black Hole, the 1880 legislature called for a three-man commission, appointed by the governor, to "select a site, to receive plans and specifications for the location and erection of a Branch Penitentiary . . . and to examine into the construction, equipment, government, and discipline of prisoners in other states . . . for the purpose of adopting the best and most practical plan" for Kentucky's new facility.[4] A few days after Blackburn signed the law, he appointed Maysville attorney and former Congressman R.

H. Stanton, General H. B. Lyons of Eddyville, and editor and Judge William M. Beckner of Clark County as the commissioners, and a few weeks thereafter the three men commenced their study of American prisons.

In June 1880 Stanton, Lyons, and Beckner visited the Ohio State Penitentiary, a facility they decided "suffered much from the fluctuation of Ohio politics," and then attended the annual Conference of Charities and Corrections at Cleveland. At the conference they heard "intelligent" discussions on the administration of justice and management of prisons by "professional philanthropists and sentimental humanitarians" engaged in penology.[5] After the Cleveland meeting the men visited institutions in Massachusetts and New York, and later in the summer toured prisons in Indiana, Illinois, and Tennessee. They were favorably impressed with the three-level progressive classification of prisoners, an adaptation of the Irish System, used at New York's Elmira Reformatory. Every prisoner entering Elmira was assigned to the middle plateau. Twice a year his record received careful scrutiny and the malefactor was then detained, demoted, or promoted as his behavior warranted. After six months of praiseworthy behavior in the top level, the prisoner was paroled, providing he went to work and conducted himself "honestly, soberly, and decently" and received good reports from his employer and parole officer. If he failed to comply with the terms of probation, he was returned to the reformatory and again had to earn his right for future privileges. This system, the commissioners believed, should be used at Kentucky's proposed prison. The physical plant of the planned institution, they decided, would be similar to the new reformatory at Joliet, Illinois.

Following visits to various areas of the state, the committee selected sites at Bowling Green and Eddyville as the most suitable locations for the branch penitentiary. They then hired a Louisville architectural firm, H. P. McDonald and Brothers, to study the areas, prepare plans, and estimate costs for the new facility. The proposed Bowling Green site was on a river bluff three-fourths of a mile from the center of town and about one mile from the town's steamboat landing. Served by the river and the Louisville and Nashville Railroad, the area abounded in good brick clay, building stone, and many other supplies needed for the construction of a prison; skilled craftsmen, mechanics, and special machinery were available at the nearby town. A prison could be built at Bowling Green for $20,000 less than at Eddyville, the Louisville firm advised, but they pointed to several disadvantages which they believed made the Warren County site undesirable. Coal would have to be imported, probably from the Eddyville area; the site was not conducive to agricultural endeavor and thus farm work and a prison vegetable garden would be impossible; Bowling Green was farther than Eddyville from the markets for prison-manufactured goods; and the "relative amount of mischief that would be done the community in which a penitentiary is established, both by unsettling its labor market and the sojourn of released prisoners within its borders" rendered the southcentral Kentucky site inappropriate.[6]

The eighty-acre farm of ex-Senator Willis B. Machen near Eddyville, a village of 600, was more suitable for the proposed prison, the Louisville firm advised. It adjoined the Elizabeth and Paducah Railroad, was within 2,000 yards of the Cumberland River and was 116 feet above the river's low-water mark. A healthy area, conducive to agricultural endeavor and in immediate proximity to immense stores of coal, iron, lumber, brick clay, and building stone, Eddyville was sufficiently remote from a town of any size and ideal for a prison.

Plans drawn by McDonald called for a wall and buildings of brick and Kentucky limestone. The main building would house the offices of the warden, assistant warden, physician, and guards as well as the laundry, chapel, hospital, storerooms, and cells for women. Other proposed buildings included a warden's house, an engine house, a workshop and two cell houses, each containing a schoolroom, bathroom, 320 regular cells, and 12 solitary cells. McDonald estimated the cost of the proposed plant at $565,122, a figure that might be reduced by half with the use of convict labor. The plan was submitted to the 1881-1882 legislature but received very little attention. Contracting the overflow population at the Frankfort prison to work on railroads had relieved its major problem and reduced the public condemnation of the "Black Hole." There was no need, economy-minded lawmakers decided, to spend half a million dollars to improve the lot of the state's "degenerates." Despite Blackburn's public and private pleas, the legislators refused to consider the expensive plan. However, as convicts died from exposure, ill-treatment, and accidents, and as public outcry against the use of convicts on public projects increased, subsequent legislators reconsidered the plan that Blackburn proposed earlier. In 1884 the state's lawmakers appropriated funds for the facility at Eddyville, but the Eddyville Penitentiary failed to meet Blackburn's goal—a place from which rehabilitated felons returned to society as useful and law-abiding citizens.

To prevent the Frankfort prison from again becoming overcrowded, to rescue mistreated convicts from the inhuman conditions associated with the railroad camps, and perhaps to keep the penitentiary question before the voting public, Blackburn continued his liberal pardoning policy throughout his administration. During his four years in office, "Lenient Luke" issued more than 1,000 pardons, a small percentage of the requests he received but nevertheless a substantial number. As families and friends of convicts learned of the governor's tender heart, they deluged him with pardon requests, and Blackburn considered each one carefully. One of the requests, presented by the tearful, lisping children of a convicted wife-murderer sentenced to die on the scaffold, apparently moved the humanitarian to tears, but not enough to grant a pardon or reprieve; Blackburn believed the man was guilty as charged and that the court was justified in its sentence. On another occasion, tears of a widowed mother proved effective. The penniless woman traveled from Covington to Frankfort to present a personal plea to the governor. Unable to see the busy executive, she sought out Mrs. Blackburn, who heard her pitiful story, provided her with food and lodging, and made arrangements for her to meet with the governor and an attorney. The woman convinced them that her son had been the scapegoat in an accidental shooting of a friend and was convicted on circumstantial evidence. The governor granted a pardon. Julia later recalled that it was "the most joyful news that any mother ever received—the pardon of her boy behind bars."[7]

Not all young men were so lucky. A few months before he left office, Blackburn received petitions signed by many influential persons requesting a pardon for Thomas Crittenden, the twenty-nine-year-old grandson of Kentucky's beloved John J. Crittenden. Indicted for killing a black man during a drunken brawl, Crittenden came to trial in April 1883. Blackburn attended part of the hearing, and when the hung jury failed to return a verdict, many persons believed the governor would grant the pardon as a favor to the young man's prominent family and to the memory of his noble grandfather. But Blackburn learned of Crittenden's involvement in several other brawls while he was out on bail awaiting trial; the governor refused to interfere.

As he used his executive privilege, the press heaped abuses on the governor with unprecedented venom, and his pardoning policy became a highly emotional issue. Condemnation, reverberating from every part of the state, occasionally was more severe than the novice politician could endure. In refusing to ignore unjust and petty derision, Blackburn made himself a target for even greater abuse. The affair between the governor and the Warren County Circuit Court typified the unfavorable publicity that resulted.

The affair began after Blackburn pardoned a Mr. Doyle of Warren County prior to a jury's verdict; pretrial pardons had been approved in a much earlier Court of Appeals decision. Doyle's first trial ended with a hung jury, but the majority of the jurors believed him innocent. Blackburn's pardon, which eliminated the necessity of a retrial, was, according to someone's incorrect calculations, the twenty-first pardon granted to a Warren countian in eighteen months. The local grand jury denounced Blackburn's meddling and circulated a petition condemning his pardoning policy and claiming that he sold pardons for two dollars each. Circuit Judge William L. Dulaney also delivered from his bench a scathing denunciation of the governor and suggested that there was no reason for a judge to waste his time and jeopardize his health by holding trials for persons the governor would pardon.

Enraged by the judge's tirade and the jury's petition, Blackburn vented his ire during an interview with a Louisville reporter. "Those dirty whaims [sic]," Blackburn scolded, "don't amount to anything. I dare say every mother's son of them has signed petitions praying me to pardon somebody." The governor believed that Dulaney, who "wasn't fit to be a police judge," was behind the petition.[8] Embarrassed by the affair, a group of Bowling Green residents drew up a petition defending the governor and mildly censuring the judge and the grand jury, which they claimed was made up of Republicans. Blackburn answered that he did not need "vindication by the good people of Warren County against ignorant and wicked columinators [sic]."[9] The *Bowling Green Democrat* tried to make amends by praising Blackburn's humane interests but added that "the only objection our people find . . . [is] his wreckless [sic] use of pardons." Newspapers across the state had a field day with the entire conflict. They condemned Blackburn for his "base profanity," the judge for his refusal to hold trials, the jury for its meddling into matters that were none of its business, and the Bowling Green paper for its inability to spell.[10]

Blackburn's involvement in another type of name-calling apparently resulted from a misunderstanding or misquotation. W. F. Walton, editor of the *Stanford Interior Journal*, had been very critical of the governor's pardons and venomous about his refusal to answer many of the diatribes hurled at him by various papers. In March of 1882 a man named Ruppert was arrested for pulling a gun on Walton. Shortly thereafter someone suggested that Blackburn ought to offer a pardon to the would-be assassin. The comment, probably made in jest, was repeated, quoted, and misquoted. The *Louisville Commercial* claimed Blackburn told Ruppert that if he had killed the "G-d d----d son-of-a-b----, I would pardon you right now." In his paper Walton accused the "old loon" of offering a reward to anyone who would shoot any newspaper editor or reporter. The puerile statements prompted more criticism but also some defense of the governor. A Stanford politician, speaking before an audience at Lancaster, told his listeners that the old governor was "a man among men . . . he is not afraid of the Devil. . . . I tell you, gentlemen, when God made Luke Blackburn, He cast him in His proudest mold."[11]

Cries against Blackburn's liberal use of his executive privilege increased when it was suggested that the governor and the secretary of state charged two dollars for every pardon granted, an unjust but often repeated statement. The *Muhlenberg Echo* told its readers that people "marched" into the secretary of state's office, "planked down their two dollars and received their pardons." The *Danville Advocate* went so far as to criticize the "tenderhearted governor" for holding up a pardon for a Boyle County burglar while his wife "scratched up two dollars," and the same paper speculated that the governor and secretary of state netted over $40,000 on pardons during Blackburn's first two years in office.[12] The *Courier-Journal* and the *Yeoman* valiantly attempted to explain that no charges were made for pardons but that the state law required the assistant secretary of state to collect a two-dollar fee for each fine-remission. Most of Blackburn's remissions were granted to victims of circumstances, ignorance, or prejudice, but these acts of mercy, too, were censured, for each remission represented a loss of income to the state.

The accusation about the sale of pardons eventually died down, but in 1883 rumors circulated that "pardon brokers" found Blackburn's "wholesale pardons" lucrative. In regard to the pardon brokers and Blackburn's liberal pardoning policy, the *Russellville Herald-Enterprise* provided a constructive suggestion. A board of pardons should be created, the Simpson County paper suggested, to assist the governor in the exercise of clemency. He received too many requests to review all of them adequately and justly.

One of the often-repeated complaints against Blackburn's use of executive privilege was that the state's increasing crime rate resulted from the pardoning of murderers, rapists, and thieves. On March 14, 1882, James Breathitt of Christian County introduced a resolution into the house labeling this charge a "miserable sham." Breathitt believed that the pardons were granted in such cases "as present a state of circumstances that are *peculiar*, by reason of which the general laws in their operation work an unusual hardship for the promotion, and not the defeat, of the ends of justice." To prove his point, Breathitt requested that the secretary of state furnish the house with a complete transcript of pardons, respites, and remissions of fines granted by the governor as well as "any other facts which he may deem of sufficient interest to report."[13] The governor did not have to account for his actions to the legislature, and thus the request was of questionable constitutionality. Nevertheless, Secretary of State James Blackburn compiled a lengthy report which contained the names of pardoned convicts, the petitions presented to the governor in their behalf, and the governor's reason for granting each request.

The report, covering 845 pardons granted during Blackburn's first eighteen months in office, reveals that most of the pardons were granted at the request of judges, juries, or large numbers of community residents who believed that an injustice had occurred. Young offenders thirteen to twenty-one years of age and elderly disabled convicts also received many of the pardons. Three were granted to men who had completed their sentences but because of incompetent prison administration were still incarcerated, and several dozen whose sentences expired within a few days received pardons to restore their citizenship. A random selection of the pardons illustrates the type of malefactors to whom Blackburn granted executive clemency:

111

An elderly man sentenced for killing his son-in-law in self-defense: His jury requested that he be permitted to return to the community to care for his young, motherless children who were farmed out among strangers.

An elderly man sentenced for murder: He had lost one arm and had another severely mangled in an accident resulting from malfunctioning prison machinery.

A one-armed Negro whose diseased leg was amputated in the prison hospital: His former master promised to care for the incapacitated man for the remainder of his life.

A man sentenced for raping his stepdaughter: His jury later discovered that his wife and stepdaughter had sold all of his property and were operating a bawdy house. It now believed the rape charge had been levied to gain his property.

A Negro sentenced for bigamy: Blackburn granted the unsolicited pardon because he believed the man's crime "grew out of the loose manner in which the colored people of this State were taught to regard the marital relations prior to emancipation."[14]

A fifteen-year-old boy found guilty of storehouse breaking: Blackburn feared the youth would be "ruined in body and morals" by association with hardened criminals.[15]

A man sentenced for being a second in a duel fought thirteen years prior to his conviction.

Three hundred and ninety Regulators from Lawrence County: The district judge requested the pardons and assured the governor that these "lawless people" voluntarily surrendered to him and took an oath that they would never again disturb the peace.

The General Assembly received the pardon report the day before its April 1882 adjournment; in the lawmakers' haste to depart for home, they neglected to arrange for the report's publication. The following December, after other state documents were printed and distributed, someone remembered the pardon report and asked about its fate. Several newspapers suggested that it had been thrown away so that those who signed the many petitions included in it, and later "venomously criticized" the governor for exercising his right, would not be embarrassed. The *Hartford Herald*, one of the governor's most truculent critics, predicted that the report would never be published for it was "too black a showing against our 'great' and 'good' Samaritan."[16] The *Louisville Commercial* reasoned that state officials conspired to destroy the missing document, but the *Yeoman*, whose editor also served as state printer, admitted that because he estimated the publication cost at $5,000 he deemed it advisable to await authorization before printing it. To the suggestion that Blackburn use his own funds to finance the report's publication, the *Carlisle Mercury* reminded its readers that Blackburn's lack of interest in a political career rendered him unconcerned about the opinions and prejudices of uninformed persons. Because of the hullabaloo over the "lost document," the treasurer approved the expenditure and the state printer published the 557-page report and released 624 copies of it in mid-February of 1883. Nevertheless, criticism of Blackburn's pardons continued.

By the spring of 1883 Blackburn was so unpopular with the press that few kind words could be found about him. Even those papers that earlier had defended him now either joined his critics or simply remained silent about his activities. One of the harshest comments on the governor, which numerous other papers echoed, appeared in the *Hartford Herald*. The Hartford editor thanked God that "his fraudulency" would soon pass into oblivion except in the "foggy memory" of cutthroats, murderers, and blacklegs. The *Owensboro Record*, which generally referred to Blackburn as an "old imbecile," also praised the Deity that Blackburn would no longer be around to harm the state.

The most unbecoming display of disapproval, however, punctuated the 1883 Democratic nominating convention in Louisville. Outgoing governors traditionally made a few comments about the accomplishments of their administration, but when Blackburn attempted to defend his pardoning policy, boos and catcalls drowned out his words. In anger he shouted above the din that he had a right to defend himself. His interest in the penitentiary and its inhabitants was genuine, he said, and anyone who said he was guilty of abusing his executive privilege or of corruption was a "liar—a base, infamous liar." Because of the deafening clamor, the governor cut short his speech and thanked those "who have paid me attention, and as for the rowdies, I have a perfect contempt." Few members of the audience heard him. The *Oldham Era* shamed the politicians who "combined to cry down his administration."[17]

On September 5, 1883, Blackburn delivered his last speech as governor before a large crowd assembled in Frankfort to celebrate the inauguration of his successor, J. Proctor Knott. The listeners were polite this time, but Blackburn's remarks sounded like those of a wounded man who feared more jeers. In referring to opposition to his pardons, he noted that "in any state there are the scullions of defamation who, the more ignorant they are to the cause that leads to acts, the more vituperative they become and appear to take delight in trying to pull down those who have the manliness to do what they believe is right even though it be in the face of some passing popular clamor."[18] With the swearing in of Knott, the executive who had pushed through the first major reform since the Civil War relinquished his office. He had been elected on a wave of public gratitude and admiration four years earlier; the state's politicos, angered by his lack of discretion, his liberal pardons, and his support of an unpopular and expensive cause, now experienced relief that his administration was over.

Blackburn left Frankfort the day after Knott's inauguration and visited a Virginia resort for a brief rest before returning to Louisville to attend the National Conference of Charities. At the meeting Blackburn received public praise from guest speaker, novelist-reformer George W. Cable, for his efforts to erase the horrors of the lessee system and to improve the general welfare of the state's charges. A few weeks thereafter Blackburn attended a similar conference in Saratoga, New York, where he again was lauded for his reforms at the Kentucky Penitentiary. To his friends, the former governor declared that despite the scorn heaped upon him because of his pardons, he would grant all but one of them again.

A few months after Blackburn's return to his apartment at the Galt House, he leased from the city of Louisville six acres of land adjoining Cave Hill cemetery and founded a sanitarium for the "treatment of mental disease and nervous disorders."[19] Although he desired to continue aiding his fellowman, the old physician's declining health impeded the hospital's success. In January of 1887 the Blackburns returned to Frankfort. He had "come home to die and be received into the bosom of his best loved city," the ex-governor told a friend. Eight months later, following a lengthy illness, Blackburn slipped into a coma from which he never recovered. He died September 14, 1887.[20]

He had angered the politicians, but the little people respected Blackburn's willingness to aid those who needed his help, and they flocked to Frankfort to attend his last rites. State offices and all businesses in Frankfort closed on the afternoon of the funeral; flags flew at half-mast over the Arsenal and State House, and buildings in Versailles, Hickman, and Fulton were draped with black crepe. Following an impressive ceremony at Frankfort's Episcopal Church, Blackburn's remains were interred in the Frankfort Cemetery on a hillside overlooking the Kentucky River.

On May 27, 1891, the state unveiled a large granite monument at Blackburn's grave. The dedication address, delivered by the eloquent Basil Duke, praised the former governor but mentioned his political shortcomings. Duke called Blackburn "the frankest man I ever knew. He never left you in doubt as to what he thought or meant. . . . He was too ready, perhaps, to join controversy with those who expressed a desire for that sort of entertainment, but he never by word or deed offended one who did not first offer him provocation, and he never found fault with—rarely indeed, took issue with—those whom he loved." Duke praised Blackburn's humanitarian endeavors as physician, public health officer, and governor. Concerning his "frequent exercise of the pardoning power, a prerogative employed too frequently, many people honestly thought," Duke explained that it was "dedicated by that mercy which urges forgiveness of the unfortunates who err and fall under temptation."[21]

Blackburn's monument is overshadowed by larger, more ornate stones marking the final resting places of Kentucky's pioneers, statesmen, and warriors. Its lengthy, rather flowery inscription, which Duke intended as a salute to "the life and conduct of which his friends are proud and which his people should remember," is a touching tribute to the man who defied disease and disapproval in his efforts to help those unable to help themselves.[22] The monument's brass plaque depicts a parable recorded in the New Testament by the "beloved physician" Luke—the memorable deed of the Good Samaritan.

Notes

Chapter 1

1. Charles H. Caldwell to George Hayward, Nov. 25, 1832, Special Collections, Margaret I. King Library, University of Kentucky.

2. J. O. Harrison to Jilson Harrison, July 12, 1833, Micajah Harrison Papers, Kentucky Historical Society, Frankfort.

3. "Epidemic Cholera: An Eclectic, Miscellaneous and Clinical Review," *Western Journal of Medical and Physical Sciences* 7 (April-June 1833): 91.

4. *Niles Weekly Register* 44 (July 6, 1833): 305.

5. [Jefferson J. Polk], *Autobiography of Dr. J. J. Polk* . . . (Louisville, Ky., 1867), p. 33.

6. Luke Prior [*sic*] Blackburn, "Cholera Maligna" (M.D. thesis, 1835, Transylvania University), pp. 4, 15.

7. *Kentucky Gazette*, July 4, 1835.

8. Louisville *Courier-Journal*, Sept. 17, 1887.

9. Ella Blackburn to Lavinia Blackburn, n.d., Blackburn Family Papers, Special Collections, Margaret I. King Library, microfilm.

10. *Natchez Weekly Courier*, June 16, 1847.

11. Ella Blackburn to Lavinia Blackburn, Oct. 1, Nov. 1, 1846; Luke P. Blackburn to Lavinia Blackburn, Oct. 10, 1846, Blackburn Family Papers.

12. Ella Blackburn to Lavinia Blackburn, Dec. 18, 1846, June 2, 1847, ibid.

13. *Congressional Record*, 30th cong., 1st sess., July 18, 1848, p. 949.

14. *Mississippi Free Trader*, July 29, 1852.

15. Ibid., Aug. 18, 1848.

16. William Ranson Hogan and Edwin Adams Davis, eds., *William Johnson's Natchez: The Ante Bellum Diary of a Free Negro*, 2

vols., (Port Washington, N.Y., 1968), 2: 627; *Natchez Daily Courier*, Sept. 5, 19, 1848.

17. *Natchez Daily Courier*, Nov. 2, 1848.

18. Ella Blackburn to Lavinia Blackburn, Nov. 27, 1853, Blackburn Family Papers.

19. Joseph Statton, *Memorial of a Quarter-Century's Pastorate* (Philadelphia, 1869), pp. 55-56.

20. Ella Blackburn to Lavinia Blackburn, July [n.d.], Sept. 17, Nov. 13, 27, 1853, Blackburn Family Papers.

21. *Natchez Daily Courier*, Oct. 3, 1854.

22. Ibid., Oct. 24, 1854. It should be noted that neither the 1848 nor the 1854 epidemic was as severe in New Orleans and elsewhere as the one in 1853.

23. *Report of the Sanitary Commission of New Orleans on the Epidemic Yellow Fever of 1853* (New Orleans, 1854), p. 535.

24. John A. Quitman to Henry R. Jackson, May 7, 1857; _____ to Dr. Marshall Hale, May 16, 1857; D. S. Rivers to Luke P. Blackburn, Dec. 9, 1857, Churchill Family Papers, Filson Club, Louisville.

25. Abby Zane to Luke P. Blackburn, Nov. 20, [1859?], ibid.

26. Churchill Family Papers.

Chapter 2

1. Luke P. Blackburn to Sterling Price, Aug. 20, 1862, General and Staff Officers Papers, War Department Collection, Confederate Records, National Archives, Washington, D.C.

2. *Mississippi Daily Advertiser*, Feb. 3, 1863.

3. Luke P. Blackburn to _____, May 3, 1863, General and Staff Officers Papers, War Department Collection, Confederate Records.

4. Luke P. Blackburn to Dabney H. Maury, June 23, 1863, Churchill Family Papers.

5. Col. Mundy [?] to Julia Churchill, July 21, 1863, ibid.

6. James Blackburn to Emily Blackburn, Oct. 2, 1861, quoted in Frank Moore, ed., *The Rebellion Record: A Diary of American Events, with Documents, Narratives, Illustrative Incidents, Poetry, Etc.*, 10 vols. (New York, 1862-1868), 3: 44. James Blackburn's cold-blooded comment would prevent his appointment in 1885 as collector of revenue for Lexington.

7. JoAnn Carrigan, "Yankee versus Yellow Fever in New

Orleans, 1862-1866," *Civil War History* 9 (Sept. 1963): 249, 250.

8. Ibid., pp. 253, 249.

9. "American Consular Reports—Civil War Period," *Bermuda Historical Quarterly* 19 (Spring 1962): 25.

10. Thomas E. Taylor, *Running the Blockade: A Personal Narrative of the Adventures, Risks, and Escapes during the American Civil War* (London, 1896), p. 130.

11. "Consular Reports," p. 26.

12. *Bermuda Royal Gazette*, May 30, 1865.

13. *New York Times*, May 21, 1865.

14. Ibid., May 26, 1865.

15. Ibid.

16. Ibid.

17. *Montreal Gazette*, May 27, 1865; *New York Times*, May 30, 1865.

18. C. L. Leathers to James Brown, Apr. 28, 1866, Amnesty Papers—Kentucky, Records of the Adjutant General's Office, 1780-1917, National Archives, Washington, D.C.

19. Luke P. Blackburn to Andrew Johnson, Sept. 4, 1867, Andrew Johnson Presidential Papers, Manuscript Division, National Archives, microfilm, ser. 1, reel 28.

20. Seward's letter quoted in *New York Times*, Sept. 26, 1867.

21. *Cincinnati Gazette*, Sept. 18, 1879.

Chapter 3

1. *Courier-Journal*, May 20, 1873.

2. Ibid., Sept. 16, 1873.

3. J. M. Keating, *The Yellow Fever Epidemic of 1878* (Memphis, Tenn., 1879), p. 383. This study includes a lengthy account of the 1873 epidemic.

4. Ibid., p. 385.

5. D. A. Quinn, *Heroes and Heroines of Memphis; Or, Reminiscences of the Yellow Fever Epidemic That Affected the City of Memphis during the Autumn Months of 1873, 1878, and 1879* (Providence, R.I., 1887), pp. 107-10.

6. Ibid., p. 107.

7. *Courier-Journal*, Oct. 28, 1873.

8. Quoted ibid., Oct. 23, Nov. 25, 1877; *Journal of the Senate of Kentucky, 1878* (Frankfort, 1878), p. 469.

9. Jefferson Davis to J. Proctor Knott, Jan. 22, 1878, in Dun-

bar Rowland, ed., *Jefferson Davis, Constitutionalist*, 10 vols. (Jackson, Miss., 1923), 7:486.

10. Luke P. Blackburn to Jefferson Davis, Feb. 26, 1878, quoted ibid., 8: 118-19; *Courier-Journal*, Feb. 11, Mar. 8, 1878; Basil W. Duke, *Reminiscences of Basil W. Duke, C.S.A.* (New York, 1911), p. 481.

11. *Shelbyville Sentinel*, May 8, 1878.

12. Frankfort *Kentucky Yeoman*, May 1, 1878; *Courier-Journal*, June 10, 1878.

13. *Courier-Journal*, Mar. 8, 1878; *Kentucky Yeoman*, July 9, 1878.

14. *Journal of the House of Representatives of Kentucky, 1878* (Frankfort, 1878), p. 1078.

15. *Courier-Journal*, Aug. 21, 26, 1878.

16. *Louisville Medical News* 6(Sept. 7, 1878): 115.

17. *Courier-Journal*, Oct. 7, 1878.

18. Duke, *Reminiscences*, p. 482; *Courier-Journal*, Aug. 21, 24, 1878.

19. J. A. Singleton, "Memorial Address on the Life, Character, and Death of Dr. John Loy Cook," *American Practitioner* 19(Mar. 1879): 185.

20. Quoted in *Kentucky Yeoman*, Oct. 5, 1878, and *Paducah Daily News*, Oct. 15, 1878.

21. Paris *True Kentuckian*, Nov. 6, 1878. The first quotation is inscribed on the medal that the western Kentucky towns presented to Blackburn. This medal and many other mementos were given to the Kentucky Historical Society shortly after the death of Mrs. Blackburn.

22. Ibid., Jan. 22, 1879.

23. *Glasgow Press*, Mar. 20, 1879.

24. John Cox Underwood to Clarence McElroy, Nov. 19, 1878, McElroy Collection, Kentucky Library, Western Kentucky University; *Courier-Journal*, Nov. 19, 1878.

25. Quoted in *Courier-Journal*, Jan. 17, 1879.

26. Ibid., Jan. 18, 1879.

27. Ibid., Jan. 28, 1879.

28. John Cox Underwood to Clarence McElroy, Dec. 31, 1878, McElroy Collection.

29. *Courier-Journal*, Mar. 26, 1879.

30. Quoted in *True Kentuckian*, Dec. 11, 1878.

31. *Courier-Journal,* June 11, 1879.

32. *Louisville Medical News* 7(May 10, 1879): 220; *Courier-Journal,* May 3, June 5, 1879. A third candidate, C. W. Cook representing the National (Greenback) party, would receive about 8.6 percent of the votes, but apparently he did little campaigning. Most of Kentucky's Greenback party supporters voted Democratic in state elections.

33. *Lexington Weekly Transcript,* June 14, 1879.

34. *Courier-Journal,* June 6, July 8, 1879; *South Kentuckian,* May 20, 1879.

35. *South Kentuckian,* May 6, 1879.

36. Quoted in *Cincinnati Gazette,* Aug. 5, Sept. 1, 1879.

37. Ibid., Oct. 2, 1879.

38. *Courier-Journal,* July 30, Aug. 10, 1879.

39. Catlettsburg *Central Methodist,* July 19, 1879.

40. Harriet R. Holman, ed., "Journal of Thomas Nelson Page," *Register of the Kentucky Historical Society* 68(Jan. 1970): 7.

Chapter 4

1. *Courier-Journal,* Sept. 3, 1879.

2. Ibid.

3. Ibid.

4. Owensboro *Semi Weekly Messenger and Examiner,* Mar. 26, 1880.

5. *Courier-Journal,* Jan. 3, 1880.

6. *New York Times,* Dec. 19, 1881.

7. *Courier-Journal,* Sept. 30, 1880.

8. Ibid., Dec. 10, 1880.

9. *Louisville Commercial,* Aug. 24, 1879; *Breckinridge News,* Sept. 10, 1879; quoted in *Paducah Daily News,* Aug. 22, 1879.

10. *Courier-Journal,* Jan. 25, 15, 1880.

11. A. F. Duncan to Clarence McElroy, Aug. 6, 1881, McElroy Collection.

12. Executive Journal of Luke P. Blackburn, Jan. 1, 1880, Governors' Papers, Kentucky Historical Society; *Journal of the House of Representatives of Kentucky, 1880* (Frankfort, 1880), p. 39.

13. *Journal of the House, 1880,* pp. 54-55.

14. Ibid., p. 57.

15. *Courier-Journal,* Apr. 22, 1880.

16. *Report of the Adjutant General, State of Kentucky, to the Commander in Chief, for the Year 1880, Kentucky Documents, 1880* (Frankfort, 1880), p. 6.

17. *Kentucky Yeoman*, Nov. 1, 1881; *Glasgow Times*, Nov. 10, 1881.

18. *Report of the Adjutant General, State of Kentucky, to the Commander in Chief, for the Year 1882-1883, Kentucky Documents, 1882* (Frankfort, 1882), p. 7.

19. C. E. Bowman to Clarence McElroy, Oct. 17, 1879, McElroy Collection.

Chapter 5

1. *Report on the Penitentiary, Kentucky Documents, 1879* (Frankfort, 1879), p. 15.

2. *Paducah Daily News*, Oct. 31, 1879.

3. Ibid.

4. *Journal of the House of Representatives of Kentucky, 1880*, pp. 42, 50.

5. Ibid., p. 221.

6. *Report of the Special Committee on the Penitentiary to the Senate, February 26, 1880, Kentucky Documents, 1880* (Frankfort, 1880), pp. 9, 35, 36, 72.

7. Ibid., p. 53; *Kentucky Yeoman*, Mar. 13, 1880.

8. *Cincinnati Commercial*, Apr. 10, 1880.

9. *Courier-Journal*, Jan. 31, 1880; Anna Dale to Luke Blackburn, Feb. 3, 1880, Churchill Family Papers.

10. *Courier-Journal*, Apr. 16, 1880.

11. Ibid., May 5, 1880.

12. *Louisville Commercial*, Apr. 18, 1882.

13. *Report of the Directors and Officers of the Kentucky Penitentiary, Kentucky Documents, 1882* (Frankfort, 1882), p. 16.

14. Ibid., p. 18.

15. Minute Book of the Commissioners of the Kentucky Penitentiary, 1880-1892, Kentucky State Archives, Frankfort, July 17, 1882.

16. *Report of the Directors and Officers of the Kentucky Penitentiary, 1882*, p. 18.

17. C. R. Mason to Harry I. Todd, Nov. 24, 1882, Todd Family Papers, Filson Club.

18. Harry I. Todd to _____, Feb. 20, 1884, ibid.

19. Physician's Record Book, Kentucky Penitentiary, 1880-1892, March 21, 1881, quoted in Robert G. Crawford, "A History of the Kentucky Penitentiary System, 1865-1937" (Ph.D. diss., University of Kentucky, 1955), p. 193. The Physician's Record Book apparently is among the few nineteenth-century records still housed at LaGrange Reformatory.

20. Physician's Record Book, July 11, 1883, quoted ibid., p. 194.

21. Minute Book of the Commissioners of the Kentucky Penitentiary, June 11, 1881.

22. Lucien V. Rule, *City of Dead Souls* (Louisville, Ky., 1920), preface [n.p.].

23. Ibid.

24. Quoted in *Kentucky Yeoman*, June 19, 1883.

25. *Report of the Directors and Officers of the Kentucky Penitentiary, 1882*, p. 9.

26. W. T. Price, *Without Scrip or Purse* (Louisville, Ky., 1882), p. 357; *Courier-Journal*, June 12, 1882.

27. Price, *Without Scrip or Purse*, p. 358.

28. *Kentucky Yeoman*, Mar. 28, 1882.

29. Ibid.

30. *Report of Committee to Investigate Conditions of Convicts, Kentucky Documents, 1882* (Frankfort, 1882), p. 13.

31. *Kentucky Yeoman*, Aug. 28, 1883.

Chapter 6

1. *Journal of the House of Representatives of Kentucky, 1880*, pp. 46-47.

2. Ibid., p. 46.

3. Ibid., p. 50.

4. Ibid.; *Acts of Kentucky, 1880* (Frankfort, 1880), p. 159.

5. *Report of the Branch Penitentiary Commissioners of Kentucky to the General Assembly, Kentucky Documents, 1881* (Frankfort, 1881), pp. 3, 4.

6. Ibid., p. 35.

7. Rule, *City of Dead Souls*, preface [n.p.].

8. *Courier-Journal*, June 9, 1881.

9. Luke P. Blackburn to Clarence McElroy, June 27, 1881, McElroy Collection.

10. *Kentucky Yeoman*, Aug. 25, 1881.

11. *Louisville Commercial*, Mar. 25, 1882; *Kentucky Yeoman*, Sept. 13, 1882.

12. Quoted in *Kentucky Yeoman*, Aug. 18, 1882.

13. *Journal of the House of Representatives of Kentucky, 1881-1882* (Frankfort, 1882), p. 997.

14. *Response of Secretary of State to the Resolution Requesting Lists of Pardons, Etc., Granted by Governor Luke P. Blackburn, Kentucky Documents, 1882* (Frankfort, 1882), p. 210.

15. Ibid., p. 226.

16. Quoted in *Kentucky Yeoman*, Jan. 6, 1883.

17. Ibid., May 19, July 24, 1883.

18. Ibid., Sept. 6, 1883.

19. Petition to the General Council, Apr. 24, 1884, Mayors of Louisville, Kentucky Papers, Filson Club.

20. *Kentucky Yeoman*, Sept. 17, 1887.

21. Bennett Young, ed., *Kentucky Eloquence: Past and Present Library of Orations, After Dinner Speeches, Popular and Classical Lectures, Addresses, and Poetry* (Louisville, 1907), pp. 147, 149.

22. Basil Duke to Julia Blackburn, n.d., Churchill Family Papers.

A Note to Readers

L UKE BLACKBURN is one of the forgotten public-health figures of the nineteenth century, and, like most of the state's governors, a neglected figure in Kentucky history. Brief sketches in the *Dictionary of American Biography* and other biographical collections, a brief, poorly researched 1934 master's thesis—these are the comprehensive studies of Blackburn to date. The paucity of personal materials about the governor-physician undoubtedly is partially responsible for the neglect. Shortly after Blackburn's death, his son, Dr. Cary Blackburn of Louisville, gave his father's papers to a Louisville historian who proposed to write the humanitarian's biography. But the biography was never written and the papers have disappeared. Most of the items in two small collections of family papers, the Blackburn Family Papers on microfilm at the Margaret I. King Library, University of Kentucky, and the Churchill Family Papers on microfilm at the Margaret I. King Library, University of Kentucky, and the Churchill Family Papers at the Filson Club, relate to other members of the family and to local happenings rather than to the activities of Luke Blackburn. The Blackburn Family Papers contain some interesting letters between the doctor's wife and his mother that are filled with gossip about Natchez.

Because of the lack of Blackburn manuscripts, contemporary newspapers and Kentucky's official documents were the most valuable source for this study. Readily available and filled with news articles pertinent to the entire state, the daily *Louisville Courier-Journal* and the tri-weekly (daily during the legislature's sessions) *Kentucky Yeoman* provided a wealth of information about Blackburn. Both newspapers contain excerpts from or quote in their entirety the speeches Blackburn and other state figures delivered during campaigns, legislative debates, and at public gatherings. They also contain items copied from small-town papers across the state, many of which are unavailable to current researchers. Both papers presented relatively unbiased opinions of Blackburn's gubernatorial activities but also related comments in other state and out-of-state newssheets, many of which viciously criticized the governor.

Kentucky's published documents provided much insight into state politics and into Blackburn's gubernatorial years. The *Journal of the House of Representatives of Kentucky* and the *Journal of the Senate of Kentucky*, published in Frankfort at the end of each legislative session, record the various bills introduced, the resolutions and short committee reports presented in each house, and the governors' addresses to the legislature. Unfortunately, the debates and speeches delivered during the sessions are not included in the journals, but many of them can be found in contemporary newspapers. Laws passed by both houses and signed by the governor are found in the *Acts of Kentucky*, also published at the end of each legislative session.

The most revealing documents about Kentucky politics and the state's general well-being are the published records of various branches of government. Bound as *Kentucky Documents* between 1840 and 1918, these reports include official statements of the state treasurer, auditor, attorney general, and commissioners of agriculture, railroads, education, and insurance; also included are the reports of the directors and boards of directors of state institutions (penitentiary, schools for the blind and deaf, hospitals for the feebleminded and mentally ill) and committee reports too lengthy to include in the house and senate journals. The institutional reports should be interpreted with care, for the directors and other officials frequently made light of problems in an effort to retain their jobs.

Among the state's unpublished documents are thousands of letters received at the executive office requesting pardons and remissions of fines. Housed at the Kentucky Historical Society, these Governors' Papers, grouped according to gubernatorial administrations, are neither indexed nor cataloged and therefore are exceedingly difficult to use. Also included in the Governors' Papers are large, leather-bound ledgers containing the hand-written journals of the legislature, the bills passed by the General Assembly, those vetoed by the governor, and those introduced but not approved by the lawmakers. Most of the latter were omitted from the published journals of the house and senate. In the Executive Journals, also part of the Governors' Papers, are recorded proclamations, appointments, pardons, fine remissions, and other executive actions.

Most of the records relating to the Kentucky Penitentiary are stored at the Kentucky State Archives in Frankfort. Many of these records concern Eddyville and the Frankfort facility at the turn of the century, but among them are several items relevant to the Blackburn administration: the Minute Book of the Commissioners of the Kentucky Penitentiary, 1880-1893; the Register of Inmates (a listing of inmates, their sentences, and the date of their release), the Hospital Register, and the Punishment Record Book.

Two studies of the Kentucky Penitentiary were quite helpful as background sources for this study. William C. Sneed, *A Report on the History and Mode of Management of the Kentucky Penitentiary from Its Origin in 1798 to March 1, 1860* (Frankfort, Ky., 1860), was published as part of the 1860 *Kentucky Documents* and as a separate volume. Sneed, a former lessee, wrote the history as a follow-up of a shorter study done for the Kentucky State Medical Society and relied heavily on the reports of earlier lessees. Robert G. Crawford, "A History of the Kentucky Penitentiary System, 1865-1937" (Ph.D. diss., University of Kentucky, 1955), provides a detailed picture of the state's penal system and the prison at Frankfort. Lucien V. Rule, *City of Dead Souls* (Louisville, 1920), is a brief history of the Old Prison South, at Jeffersonville, Indiana, but contains interesting comments about the Frankfort institution derived from Rule's correspondence with Julia Blackburn, who died a few months before the book's publication.

Although the notes for this study reflect only the sources used for direct quotations, many works helped the author acquire background knowledge and a feeling for the era in which Blackburn lived. Among those used were: Lewis Collins and Richard H. Collins, *History of Kentucky*, 2 vols. (Covington, Ky., 1874); J. Stoddard Johnson, *Memorial History of Louisville from Its First Settlement to the Year 1896*, 2 vols. (Chicago, 1896); L. F. Johnson, *The History of Franklin County, Ky.* (Frankfort, Ky., 1912); Ermina Jett Darnell, *Filling the Chinks* (Frankfort, Ky., 1966); Wm. E. Railey, *History of Woodford County* (Frankfort, Ky., 1928); Dorris C. James, *Antebellum Natchez* (Baton Rouge, La., 1968); Hambleton Tapp and James Klotter, *Kentucky: Decades of Discord, 1865-1900* (Frankfort, Ky., 1977); Robert Ireland, *Little Kingdoms: The Counties of Kentucky, 1865-1890* (Lexington, Ky., 1977); Oscar A. Kinchen, *Confederate Operations in Canada and the North: A Little Known Phase of the Civil War* (North Quincy, Mass., 1970); John Chambers, *Conquest of Cholera: America's Greatest Scourge* (New York, 1938); John Duffy, *The Sword of Pestilence: The New Orleans Yellow Fever Epidemic of 1853* (Baton Rouge, La., 1966); and articles concerning yellow fever in Hickman, Bowling Green, and Louisville in *First Annual Report of the State Board of Health of Kentucky* (Frankfort, Ky., 1878).